CELEBRATING SAINTS AND SEASONS

D1258598

celebrating
saints AND
seasons

Hundreds of Activities
for Catholic Children

·JEANNE HUNT·

ST. ANTHONY MESSENGER PRESS
Cincinnati, Ohio

Scripture passages have been taken from *New Revised Standard Version Bible,* copyright
©1989 by the Division of Christian Education of the National Council of the Churches of
Christ in the U.S.A., and used by permission. All rights reserved.

Cover and book design by Mark Sullivan
Cover image © Winterberg | Dreamstime.com

LIBRARY OF CONGRESS CATALOGING-IN-PUBLICATION DATA
Hunt, Jeanne.
Celebrating saints and seasons : hundreds of activities for Catholic children / Jeanne Hunt.
p. cm.
ISBN 978-0-86716-959-1 (alk. paper)
1. Christian saints—Juvenile literature. 2. Seasons—Juvenile literature. 3. Church year—
Juvenile literature. 4. Christian education of children. 5. Christian education—Activity
programs. 6. Catholic Church—Education. I. Title.
BX4653.H86 2010
268'.432088282—dc22
2010025601

ISBN 978-0-86716-959-1

Published by St. Anthony Messenger Press
28 W. Liberty St.
Cincinnati, OH 45202
www.AmericanCatholic.org
www.SAMPBooks.org

Printed in the United States of America.

Printed on acid-free paper.

10 11 12 13 14   5 4 3 2 1

Contents

Introduction

"For everything there is a season, and a time for every matter under heaven" says Ecclesiastes 3:1. In the daily walk with students, family, friends, and our own spirit God comes to give us eyes to see and ears to hear the patterns and movement of the sacred. *Celebrating Saints and Seasons* is a connection with ordinary things that speak to us about a deeper meaning.

God uses sunsets, apple seeds, the color red, and many more things that are all around us to teach us about the divine. This book is about experiencing the seasons and the saints as inspirations for the soul. The hope is that the days of the year will create touchstones with the divine. Rituals, prayers, and activities give classroom teachers, catechists, parents, and just plain folks a tool to connect with a spiritual energy. *Ruah* is the Hebrew word for it. It means "divine breath." The *ruah* is blowing through these pages as it encourages us to see in the seasons of the earth and the church year a cadence that brings us into rhythm with the journey of life and the circle of God's love. It all sounds rather mystical. Yet, in reality, it is simply a way of looking deeper at ordinary things that can teach us how to enter into the sacred way.

Saints and heroes give us a message of hope. In *Celebrating Saints and Seasons*, we meet them as companions on the journey. They offer their wisdom and encouragement. Their lessons and prayers give us reason to believe that the sacred way is for ordinary people. It is my hope that this book will serve as a way to make living faith tangible. It is often in the little things that we meet God. This is a book for anyone who wants to find God in the ordinary moments and holy characters of the seasons.

How to Use This Book

The activities are identified for families as (F) and schools as (S). You will also see that each month includes ways to celebrate the season and saints at home and school in prayer, activities, readings, and rituals.

JANUARY

As Christmas wanes and we tire of tinsel and hearing, "Joy to the World," the deep winter and ordinary time begin. The earth is back to the ordinary as well. Beneath the gray-and-white landscape seeds rest as we envision the life they hold. It is the time for long winter walks, cups of hot chocolate, and wrapping up in a warm blanket in front of a fireplace.

Like the seeds in the ground, our spiritual energy is at rest too. As the body slows down, our souls need to do the same. These first weeks of ordinary time give us space to reflect, to muse, to stare out the window, and think about where we are now and where we are headed in the year ahead. Silence and shorter days allow us to begin that much-needed conversation with the divine—one we may have been avoiding during the busy month of December. God's voice cannot be heard more clearly than on a clear winter night in front of a roaring fire.

Celebrate the New Year

Family Talent Show (F)

Invite friends and family to your home for an evening of untold talent. Each guest must prepare a performance for the rest to enjoy. No one is excluded from the requirement. What fun it is to watch Grandpa dance, Uncle Bob do magic tricks, and Mom play the accordion! The last moments of the year fly by as the family enjoys the talent show and learns to appreciate one another in a new way.

New Year's Eve Family Film Night (F)

Invite friends and family to share the year in film. Ask guests to bring this year's collection of family videos, slides, and photos. Share summer vacations, birthdays, and anniversaries in the closing hours of the year. This entertaining activity can be scheduled before or after a shared meal or even between the courses of a grand supper.

The New Year's Campout (F)

If you live in a temperate climate, this is a perfect occasion for a multi-family campout. If you are not the wilderness type, plan ahead to rent a big cabin in the woods, mountains, desert, or at the beach. Joining family resources keeps the expense minimal, and the time together in this outdoor adventure creates memories for a lifetime. Ring in the new year around a campfire, sharing stories of years past, hopes for the future, and joys of the present. Enjoy the company of good friends and simple pleasures.

This project takes planning, but the rewards are worth the effort. Looking forward to an inexpensive time away as the holiday season closes banishes post-Christmas doldrums that come blowing in around the end of December.

New Year's Family-First Day (F)

The Christian tradition loves new beginnings! Christ offers each of us the hope of a fresh start as often as we can say *mea culpa* and pick up the pieces. New Year's Day is centered in the hope of fresh starts. Celebrate this day with a combination of quiet reflection and exciting promise.

This is a perfect occasion to attend a morning liturgy together as a family. New Year's Day is also a holy day of obligation to celebrate the Solemnity of Mary, Mother of God. After Mass, celebrate with a family brunch. Serve a breakfast typical of a foreign cuisine. Each year surprise the house with another country's menu. It is interesting to see if the eaters can guess at what country's table they are feasting.

After the morning's activities offer family members an opportunity for quiet time: walking in the neighborhood, or watching a college football game or an old movie. It might be a perfect time to collect your thoughts about the coming year. What are your goals? What one new thing would you like to accomplish this year? What did you do last year that you would like to keep doing? Spend some time listening to the Lord's answers to such questions.

In the evening, gather around a table for which each family member has prepared one dish. Everyone must bring a contribution to the meal and must prepare it unaided. Don't bother coordinating this banquet. It's much more fun to allow creativity to take its course.

After supper, gather everyone for a time of prayer. This time should be centered on hopes for the coming year, a time of petitioning prayer. Ask everyone to prepare one petition prayer for each member of the family present. As you share these prayers of hope, light a candle for each person present as a sign of Christ's light that promises to shine through each family member throughout the coming year.

Your Family's New Year's Resolutions (F)

Making a promise to yourself to change your bad habits in the coming year is the classic invitation to failure. However, this proposition can be fun and rewarding if you invite those with you on New Year's Day to help you be accountable.

Ask all guests and family members to write down one small thing they would like to change in their lives in the next year. Then put these resolutions in sealed envelopes and place in a box to be stored with the Christmas decorations. The following year invite the guests to return to another New Year's Day supper. After supper, ask people to open their envelopes and share what they wrote and what happened. The simple exercise of making resolutions that you must be accountable for adds dimension. In addition, this exercise points out how we—especially younger members of the family—change our expectations in a year's time.

Burning the Cones (F)

Here's a twist on the tradition of New Year's resolutions that you can do if you have a fireplace. In Sweden each member of the family is given a pinecone and asked to stand in front of a burning fire and proclaim a personal vice that the pinecone represents. Hold the cone high in the air, declare the "sin," then throw the pinecone into the fire. In this way you say good-bye to your fault and begin anew.

The Family Historian (F)

On New Year's Day appoint one family member or a family team as this year's historian. The family historian collects memorable souvenirs and anecdotes of the family activities for the entire year. The historian's special talents—writing, art, photography, and so on—contribute variety to the archives. On the following New Year's Day, the historian presents the family year for all to enjoy. The keepsakes, journals, and mementos can be preserved in a box and dated for your family archives.

Preparing for Back to School (F)

On the night before school begins in the new year, give your child a final gift of the Christmas season. You can fill a supply box with fresh pencils, markers, erasers, and crayons for the morning. For your teenagers, fill a box with an assignment book, new pens, a comb, and a locker mirror. For college students returning to the dorm, give personal care products and snacks. Starting back to school after the long Christmas break is more fun with a collection of new tools.

This is also a great time to give your child a book. On winter nights, this new book can fill that quiet time before bed, or you can take some time and read this book together. Parents may want to record a story or book so that children in daycare can listen to Mom or Dad reading to them.

Creating a Junk Food Chart (F)

The new year is notorious for diet resolutions. You can make a junk food/health food chart for each person in your family. High fat and sugary snacks are great once in a while, but often these treats are eaten instead of healthy choices. Keep a record of healthy foods eaten. For every three healthy choices, the person can choose one junk food item. This simple method of making food choices teaches us to respect and care for our bodies as the Creator intended. In 1 Corinthians 10:31, Paul writes about using what we eat for the glory of God. This Scripture could be placed on the chart as a gentle reminder to make wise choices.

Adopt a Family (F)

You don't have to look far to find a needy family who could use your help. In January contact your church and ask for the name of a family struggling with a personal burden—perhaps illness or unemployment. Each month do something special for this family. You can deliver a meal or buy tickets for a sporting event or movie—something that will bring a little sunshine into their lives.

Epiphany

Epiphany King Cake (F)

You can enjoy the feast of the three kings by making a "King Cake." Bake a cake that includes a bean or small plastic infant Jesus (the size of a bean). The person who finds the bean or infant Jesus is treated like a king for the day and may choose activities and a television program to watch. In New Orleans King Cakes are not served at parties until Mardi Gras. If you get the piece of cake with the infant in it, you must host the next party.

Giving Christmas Presents in the Epiphany Style (F)

In Matthew's Gospel we hear that the wise men presented the Christ child with gold, frankincense, and myrrh. On Christmas Day each family member receives three gifts. Then each day till the feast of the Epiphany the family gathers around the tree and opens one small gift: a box of crayons for a child, a bar of special soap for Mom, a special-interest magazine for Dad, and so on. These gifts can vary in cost and importance. On the feast of the Epiphany everyone receives one last grand gift (something the receiver has been dreaming and wishing for). The evenings of Christmas become very exciting. This method of receiving creates a slower pace in which the gifts are savored and appreciated, in which there is time to affirm the giver of a gift. For young children this method eliminates the frenzy of opening a big pile of gifts and not really enjoying the objects received.

This method of receiving gifts was first practiced by a family who lived far from their extended family and would be alone in a new town for Christmas. It gives each day of the season a special meaning and creates an atmosphere of festival throughout the season. The Epiphany Christmas also teaches an important lesson about focusing on the process of giving and receiving rather than the content of the gifts.

Farewell Sunday Feast (F)
On the Sunday after Epiphany invite friends and family to join you in the closing of the Christmas feast. Take down all the decorations, play the carols for the last time, eat the last of the cookies and cheese balls. Pass a journal to your guests and invite them to record their best Christmas memory for this year. Share those memories over a simple meal of soup, salad, and bread and say a final good-bye to this wonderful feast for another year.

Saints and Heroes

January 5 • Saint John Neumann (S)
This saint, who lived from 1811 to 1860, rode his horse, Geraldine, through the wilderness of America to celebrate Mass for the people of his large diocese. On this bishop's feast, ask students to write a letter of thanks to the bishop of your diocese. Introduce yourselves to the bishop and offer him your prayers.

January 15 • Martin Luther King, Jr. (F, S)
Martin Luther King, Jr., was a prophet of equality and civil rights. His life stands as an example for all of us to seek justice for those who have suffered from bigotry. During the week of his birthday, celebrate his courageous life in thought-provoking ways.

"He Had a Dream...Do You?" Essay Contest (S)

Have a school-wide essay contest. Using Martin Luther King, Jr.'s dream for a more just world as a focus, ask students to write essays about their own dreams for justice. Announce the winners of the essay contest on King's birthday. Prizes for the winners could be a copy of King's "I Have a Dream" speech or a picture of Martin Luther King, Jr.

Peace March (S)

Organize a simple march for freedom on this day. Ask each class to design a peace banner to carry in your nonviolence march. If possible, march through your school neighborhood in quiet reverence. When you return to the school say this prayer:

> God, today we remember Martin Luther King, Jr. He lived and died for the cause of justice. He yearned for the day when all your children would be treated the same. Help us to see one another with your eyes, eyes that love equally. Help us to care with your heart, a heart that makes no separation or distinction. Help us to bring the peace and justice that Martin dreamed about to our little portion of your kingdom. Amen.

The Prejudice Hour (F, S)

On Martin Luther King, Jr.'s birthday, play this awareness game: Announce to your class or family that all brown-eyed (or another characteristic such as curly hair) people have superior qualities. The brown-eyed people are smarter, richer, better-looking, and so on. The blue- and green-eyed people are less acceptable and not as smart, rich, or capable as the wonderful brown-eyed people. Spend one hour deliberately favoring the brown-eyed people. At the end of this time, ask the blue- and green-eyed people how it felt to be treated in this manner. Ask the brown-eyed people how they felt.

January 17 • Saint Anthony of the Desert (F, S)
This saint is the patron of domestic animals. Saint Anthony spent many solitary years in the deserts of Egypt. Perhaps he befriended animals to keep him company. To commemorate his day, create a collage of cat and dog pictures to hang in the classroom. Ask students to write a poem that describes their favorite pets. At home have a party for your pet in honor of Saint Anthony. Serve hot dogs or hush puppies for dinner, or, you may want to serve only vegetarian dishes on this feast of a great animal lover! Rent a family movie about a beloved animal, for example, *Bolt* or *101 Dalmatians* for young children or *Marley and Me* for teen or adult family members.

January 20 • John F. Kennedy (F, S)
On this day in 1961 President John F. Kennedy made his famous inaugural speech in which he said, "Ask not what your country can do for you—ask what you can do for your country." Make a poster illustrating the kinds of things students can do to make the United States a better place to live. Pray for the needs of our country. At home, during dinnertime go around the table and discuss this topic, replacing the word *country* with *family*: "Ask not what your family can do for you—ask what you can do for your family." Discuss all the things the family provides for the individual, and all the ways the individual can contribute to the family.

January 24 • Saint Francis de Sales (S)
Saint Francis de Sales said, "You can catch more flies with a spoonful of honey than with a hundred barrels of vinegar." This is a day to say kind things to those you meet and to keep a smile on your face. Ask your students to smile at three strangers today and to offer three honest compliments to family and friends. Then, ask them to keep a journal of the reactions to their "honey." Share the results the next day in religion class.

Prayers

A New Year
God of new beginnings,
allow us to start over with you.
You are the Creator of infinite possibilities.
You proclaim that nothing is impossible with you!
Search my heart this holy day
for the deepest wounds,
the secret desires and dreams
that wait forgotten and unspoken,
because I dare not believe
you would listen.

On this day of renewed faith,
born again in hope,
give me the courage to speak my dreams
and place them in your hands.
Give me the grace to move on them,
to act on my desire to bring wholeness into my life.
O Weaver of dreams,
teach me to walk in hope,
living each day of this year
walking into your marvelous vision of
who I am meant to be!
Amen.

Connection: Write down three things you want to abandon this year and three things you want to take with you into this year. Each first Sunday of the month review your progress and stay on your dream course.

Good Saint Basil (for his Feast Day, January 2)

Good Saint Basil,
stir into the batter of our lives a little heavenly spice.
Ask the Spirit of all inspiration
to pepper our lives with laughter.
May we be suddenly overcome
with compassion.
Let the curry of God's justice flavor our decisions.
And most of all ask the Creator
to gift us with a touch of holy oregano
to understand that love must flavor it all. Amen.

Connection: In Italy people make a spicy bread called Basil Bread to remember to approach life with the feisty spirit of Saint Basil. Try your hand at making some spicy bread or dish this January day. A good idea is making cornbread and adding red pepper flakes to the batter. Before you break and share the bread to eat say this prayer:

Epiphany Prayer

"In the time of King Herod, after Jesus was born in Bethlehem of Judea, wise men from the East came to Jerusalem, asking, "Where is the child who has been born king of the Jews?" (Matthew 2:1–2)

Epiphany moments
slip quietly into the day.
Scintillating glimpses
of the Divine among us.
Short-sighted, we miss
our chance to see
the face of God.
Preoccupied, we focus

on the mundane
everyday tasks.
We do not see
God's revelation.
Turn us into Magi,
Miracle-maker God.
Boot us out
of the familiar
into the Holy City.
Send us to the place
where you dwell.
As we leave the ordinary
we discover the sacred,
finding our heart's delight
hidden in the midst
of your world.

Connection: What star do you need to follow in order to discover God? Set up a prayer table furnished with paper stars. Ask those present to take a star and write on the points places where they feel the presence of God.

Ask everyone to go around the circle in sequence and say each of his or her special places. Let there be a short pause between the reciting of each place.

Twelfth Night Vespers
Supplies: A chime, music to the hymn "We Three Kings" and other seasonal music for meditation, a crèche with three Magi, a candle, and a Bible.
Preparation: Place the crèche, candle, Bible in the center of your prayer space.

Leader: O God, come to our assistance.
All: O Lord, make haste to help us.

Opening Prayer

Melchior, Gaspar, and Balthasar, we join you in your walk toward the manger. Let us bring three gifts with us: the gold of discipleship, the frankincense of childlike innocence, the myrrh of unexplainable hope. *Strike the chime three times.*
Scripture: Isaiah 60:1–6

Prayer of Intercession

Response: Light from Light, shine upon us!
Leader: Christ, Bearer of Light, sanctify us, we pray…*response*
Christ, Ever-Present Lord, lead us to live the gospel, we pray… *response*
Christ, Long-Awaited Messiah, enkindle in us the fire of your love, we pray… *response*
Christ, Exalted King of Glory, give us your vision, we pray… *response*
Christ, Prince of Peace, give us the courage to work for justice, we pray… *response*
Christ, Master of Paradox, renew our belief in the mystery of faith, we pray… *response*
Christ, Sign of the Impossible, lead us into your will, we pray… *response*

Closing Prayer

Side One: Let us leave the manger with hope. Hope in the ways of the gospel, which we promise to follow.
Side Two: Let us carry the Christ with us in our daily lives, so that he may become more than a memory of Christmas devotion.
Side One: Let us be encouraged knowing that we leave the manger together and pledge to support one another through the journey of the year to come.

Side Two: Let us not forget to open our hearts and home in the spirit of this holy night.

Hymn: "We Three Kings"

Connection: On this day it is an ancient tradition to mark your door with the sign of hospitality and Epiphany. Just as Mary and Joseph welcomed the Magi, try to be a home of hospitality this year, welcoming all that enter your door, as you would welcome Christ. To remember this intention go through your house today, sprinkling water with a pine branch. Walk through the rooms asking God to cleanse and bless each space and those who will use it. To culminate this holy walk stop at your door and write above it "20C+B+M10" "20" represents this millennium, the initials stand for each of the three magus's names, and the last two digits represent the current year.

Hymn for Uphill Battles (for the Feast of Saint John Neumann, January 5)

Saint John Neumann,
We come to you because you must be the patron of uphill battles.
Everything in your life came hard.
You fought to become a priest,
leaving all you knew.
Pray that we may be willing to fight for our vocation.
You lost everything on your voyage,
but a suitcase full of books.
Pray that we may be willing to abandon
all our possessions following
God's dream for our life.
You took the miter and crosier in humility
and service.

Pray that we might walk
humbly with our God.
Oh holy one of God,
we honor your courage
and ask that you will be our special advocate
in our private uphill battles. Amen.

Connection: Saint John Neumann was a scholar and lover of
books. On his feast day have a Saint John's book exchange.
Invite a group of at least five people to bring a book they
would like to share. Let everyone explain why they loved the
book they brought, then trade them with one another.

Prayer for Plundertime (for the Feast of Saint Knut, January 13)
Saint Knut was a Scandinavian king who is famous for a winter party
called "Plundertime." He believed we were waiting too long to end
Christmas tide at Candlemas. In his day everyone was on vacation until
Candlemas. Knut said twenty days ought to do it. So, January 13 was
set aside as the day to eat up all the rest of the Christmas goodies and
get back to work. He is often pictured in rags as he sweeps away the
remnants of the feast.

> *Psalm for Plundertime*
> Good King Knut,
> Teach us your holy way
> of keeping Christmas in our hearts.
> The world is deaf to the sound of carols
> that we are obliged to sing on.
> No one turns a glance at the beauty
> of the crèche.
> Now, taken for granted
> looked over,

put away,
until another cycle has passed.
Let us plunder away
the leftovers
of the birth feast.
But, yet,
keep the holy wonder
of this sacred song
humming in our winter hearts.
You asked us to sweep away Christmas
on the outside.
May we keep the crumbs and dust
of these days
deep within. Amen.

Connection: Serve a meal of Christmas leftovers in honor of Saint Knut. After the meal, break in a new broom for your home. Use the broom to sweep away the remnants of Christmas dust that remain on your floor.

Prayer Service for Peace in Honor of Martin Luther King, Jr.
Preparation: Put a white cloth on a table along with an image of Martin Luther King and white paper doves; quietly play music suitable for meditation.

Leader: O Gentle God of Peace, come to us.
All: O God of all, make haste to help us.

Opening Prayer
Lord, today we turn our spirits to a holy peacemaker, your servant Martin. Take us away from the harsh commotion of our world and take us to the mountaintop that Martin saw. In this little respite of quiet, draw us deep within your heart. Let us meet Martin again in this place.

Guided Meditation

Allow soft music to play for a few minutes, then begin.

Leader: Imagine an awesome high place: a mountain, a grassy plateau, the scene of the Sermon on the Mount. You are standing at the foot of this grand and majestic place. *Pause.*
Others join you. See who is coming: family, friends, strangers, neighbors. Allow the spirit to help you imagine those in your life with whom you are called to share this time. *Pause.*

You begin to walk slowly up to the summit. A warm breeze is blowing. The sky seems especially blue. *Pause.* Take in the beauty of creation. You notice two figures at the crest of the hill—Martin and Jesus. *Pause.*

They are deep in conversation, sitting on a cluster of rocks. Jesus motions for you to join them. Martin grins and encourages you forward. You run the rest of the way. *Pause.*

Reader One (speaking as Jesus): My dreams for peace are meant to begin first in the heart. It is the conversion of hearts that I most deeply desire.
Reader Two (speaking as Martin): In my life, you taught me to see beyond the color of someone's skin to their heart. My friends, the dream makers, knew your thirst for peace, Lord.
Reader One (speaking as Jesus): My peace I give you. My peace I leave you. My words are living grace. I allow these resurrection words to continue to resonate throughout all time. It is for my servants to simply catch the rhythm of this Word, to allow my peace to soak softly into the soul.
Reader Two (speaking as Martin): I had so little time to teach the ways of peace. Every prophet comes for just a short time to bring your Word. My passion for justice, my mission of unity, must be passed on to those that remain.
Reader One (speaking as Jesus): The gift of peace does not require a prophet, Martin; the only requirement is a clean heart. The

work of peace is a silent witness of action, passed on one to one.

Leader: Then Jesus turns to you. With a contagious smile he lifts his hand in blessing:

You are no longer slaves but servants, peacemakers.

Martin came to show you the way.

Walk as servants of compassion,

Keepers of justice,

Advocates for unity.

He embraces you now. *Pause.* Feel his touch. He holds you for a long time. *Pause.*

You experience deep warmth within, as if your spirit is absorbed in his Spirit *Pause.*

A peace beyond all understanding pervades your being. *Pause.* He whispers something in your ear. Listen. What did he say? *Pause.* Then, very gently, Jesus releases you. *Pause.* You turn and walk home together with the others.

Allow the music to continue for another few moments.

Leader: I invite you to take a little paper dove. Write on the dove what you heard Jesus say to you during our meditation time. This message is Jesus' gift to you. Pray with these words in the days to come. Carry your dove with you this week as a reminder of this time. Ask the Holy Spirit to teach you.

Let us now exchange a greeting of peace. *Exchange a gesture of peace.* Go now, to love and serve the Prince of Peace.

All: Thanks be to God.

Evening Prayer on the Lunar New Year

Blessed Keeper of the Night,

surround us in your silent presence.

As the world darkens into winter's death,

keep our spirits warm

in the blanket of your love.

Maker of winter sky,
dazzle us with your starry wonders.
Help us to look beyond
the bounds of earth
and lift our souls
into the realm of dancing specters.
Holy watcher, guard of our sleep,
protect us through the winter night
that we might rise to the morning
with a renewed vigor for life. Amen.

Connection: Share this Lunar New Year Prayer and a warm winter beverage with a friend. Reflect with one another about favorite memories of winter nights from your past.

FEBRUARY

In the second month there is a strain of something new in the air: Winter's stillness recedes to longer days and stirrings in the earth. We sing love songs and begin to see Lent's purple on the horizon.

The church walks into Lent from the parables and miracles of ordinary time. We are called to turn around and look at ourselves with honest introspection. These are the days of restlessness when winter's wonder has become tedious and we look for a way to welcome the sun back into our grayness of spirit. We are called to declare a fast when Fat Tuesday becomes Ash Wednesday, when we leave the green pasture of ordinary time for the silence of the desert.

February 2 • Feast of the Presentation (S)

This is the day we commemorate Jesus' presentation at the Temple in Jerusalem. Luke's Gospel (2:22–38) tells us that Simeon recognized Jesus as a light to the nations. We, too, are called to be light and salt for the world. Celebrate this simple prayer service based on Matthew 5:13:

Supplies: a Bible, a bowl of unsalted treats, a bowl of salted treats, a packet of salted treats for each person. (I usually recommend peanuts, but many children have allergies, so you may need substitutions.)

Gather students in a circle. Ask each student to take an unsalted item and eat it. Then read Matthew 5:13. Pass the bowl of salted snack and ask students to eat one of these.

Discuss the following questions:

Describe the difference in the two kinds of food. Which did you like best? Why? How does the salt make the peanut taste better? Why does Jesus want us to be like salt? What does that mean?

Give each child a packet of their own salted treat to take home. Close with this prayer.

Lord, help us to be salt that flavors our world. May we bring your joy to this school, your love to our families, your care to the old and the lonely. May our friends want what we have, because they see the flavor in our lives that comes from you. Amen.

Candlemas Day (February 2) (F)

The Feast of the Presentation is also called Candlemas Day. It is a traditional day to bless the candles we use in church. Blessed candles are used in our homes as quiet lights of prayer. In the midst of storms, illness, and special needs, Catholics traditionally light blessed candles to symbolize their prayer for God's care. Remember this day with a pillar candle to be used as a "family victory candle." Every time a family member experiences a victory, light this candle for the evening meal. Light your family candle in celebration when someone gets a good grade on a difficult test, makes the basketball team, gets a promotion, recovers from an illness, and so on.

Groundhog Day (February 2) (S)

Groundhog Day traditionally is the first announcement of the hope of spring. If the groundhog doesn't see his shadow, spring is on the way. Make shadow puppets to celebrate this day. Shine a light behind your hands and move your hands and fingers to make shadow animals on the wall.

During school recess, play a game of shadow tag in honor of the groundhog. The person who is "it" tries to use his or her shadow to tag another person's shadow.

Valentine's Day

This is a day to celebrate love. There are many opinions concerning the origins of this day. Some say it comes from a Roman fertility feast; some believe it is linked to Saint Valentine, an early Roman martyr. Others trace its beginnings to the old English belief that the birds choose their mates on this day. Whatever the source of this celebration, it offers us a chance to brighten the winter with words of love. The following suggestions offer new ways to say "I love you."

Most Loving Person of the Year (F, S)

As a class or family, nominate one person who showed unselfish love in the last year. Send this person a handmade certificate naming him or her the Most Loving Person of the Year. Express your admiration and tell the award winner why he or she was chosen.

Secret Valentine Pal (F, S)

Choose a name of a family member or class member and prepare a surprise treat for that person on this day. This could be a box of candy, a flower, a handmade card, or a new book with a little note that says, "From your secret pal with love!"

Valentine Poem (F, S)

Write a poem each year to someone you love. Even if you are not a poet, the creative juices might be sparked by your love. Mothers and fathers can write little poems to their children. Encourage children to write poems to their grandparents, aunts, uncles, or siblings.

In the classroom announce a love poem contest. Recruit a judge from outside the class or school and announce the winners on this day. Display the entries in the hall or publish the winners in the church bulletin or school newsletter.

Making Valentines (F)

Gather paper, doilies, stickers, glue, markers, and crayons. Then plan an evening or weekend before Valentine's Day to create your own cards. These handmade love notes will mean so much more to the receiver than the commercial version.

Valentine's Day Vacation (F)

Use this winter feast to get away from the ordinary. Surprise your spouse with a night at a hotel. Enjoy an evening of quiet intimacy. In the morning ask the babysitter to bring the children for brunch and a swim in the hotel pool. This winter vacation splash may be just what you need to lift your spirits.

Hunting for Valentines (F)
Instead of handing your valentines to each other, hide them through-out the house. Little ones love to find hidden treasures. Looking for love messages is a great activity for housebound toddlers. To keep children guessing, give clues to the whereabouts of the special treasures.

Personalized Valentine Placemats (F, S)
Make a valentine placemat for the members of your family or class. Arrange the cards each has received on a piece of lightweight poster board. Then ask family members or classmates to write qualities that make the person so lovable, such as, "likes to laugh," or "always thinks of others." Cover the placemat with contact paper.

Valentine Breakfast (F)
Serve a pink breakfast to begin love day with a bang! Add red food col-oring to pancake batter and milk. If you are a creative cook, make heart-shaped pancakes with a cookie cutter.

Special Valentine School Lunch (F)
Pack a brown bag decorated with heart stickers. Inside the bag put a love note and a special treat such as a red balloon or a red rubber ball.

Heart's Desire Dinner (F)
Plan a valentine supper made up of every family member's favorite. You can then serve the crazy combination with a sense of humor. Chocolate ice cream and gummy bears or pizza and tacos make for great fun on this day of love.

Saints and Heroes
Celebrating the Heroes of Black History Month
During this month celebrate African-Americans who have contributed to our American life. Ask children to choose one of the people on the list below (or someone of their own choice) and create a poster, mobile, or poem about this person. Each day of the month one figure could be presented. Here are some suggestions:

February 1— Birthday of poet Langston Hughes

February 4— Birthday of Rosa Parks

February 5— Louis Lautier admitted to National Press Club and birthday of baseball player Hank Aaron

February 7— Birthday of composer Eubie Blake

February 9— Birthday of author Alice Walker

February 11— Harriet Tubman Day

February 12— National Association for the Advancement of Colored People (NAACP) founded by W.E.B. DuBois, Ida B. Wells, Archibald Grimké, Henry Moscowitz, Mary White Ovington, Oswald Garrison Villard, William English Walling, and Florence Kelley

February 16— Birthday of actor LeVar Burton

February 17— Birthday of singer Marian Anderson

February 19— Birthday of jazz singer Nancy Wilson

February 20— Frederick Douglass Day

February 21— Malcolm X assassinated

February 23— Birthday of educator W.E.B. DuBois

February 25— Hiram Rhodes Revels became a senator

February 27— Birthday of journalist Charlayne Hunter-Gault

February 3 • Saint Blase

This bishop of Sebastea in Armenia is the patron of sore throats. In many churches, a special blessing of throats is imparted on this day. The power of prayer and faith in healing the body is an important part of our faith tradition. Invite someone who has experienced the sacrament of the anointing of the sick to your class to tell about the experience.

February 22 • Moses (F, S)

This Old Testament saint deserves a feast day. Read about Moses' life in a children's Bible. Then make a burning bush to decorate your class or dining room table.

Paint a twiggy branch with red paint and anchor it in a solid base of Styrofoam. Tear up small pieces of red, yellow, and orange tissue paper. Crumple the paper and glue it to your bush. Add tissue randomly till the bush is a blaze of color. Make a small sign to place at the base of the bush that reads: "I Am Who Am!"

February 22 • George Washington (F)
Who cut down the cherry tree? We all know it was little George. Serve a cherry pie for dessert today. While you share the pie, talk about lying. Ask your family these questions: What commandment warns against lying? Are white lies really harmful? Tell a story of a time you got caught in a lie. How did you feel?

Prayers
Winter Psalm
O, Maker of Ice and Cold,
O, Startling Breath of Winter,
awesome and wonderful is your white extravagance.
Flying snow invades our reverie
of winter dreams.
We are blasted with your frost and ice,
piling high on the windows of our spirits.
You have made the earth
into a crystal showcase.
Praise streaks the landscape into white and gray grace.
All the earth proclaims the greatness of God!
As for us,
you delight our eyes with your white-silver palette
and never forget to keep us warm
and safe is the shelter-fire of Love Incarnate.
Winter song fills our hearts.
with delight,
We breathe this deep, cool grace

of another marvelous day.
For you are always near,
White Grace.
Surround our hearts.
May we see beyond ice
to fire. Amen.

Connection: Go for a winter walk. Smell the air. Touch the crystal ice of a branch. Observe frost on a windowpane. (If you live in a temperate climate, let your winter walk be a time to notice the small changes in the landscape. These changes are subtler, yet they let us know that creation is always in a state of flux.) Take a moment to praise God for winter. Then, come inside and enjoy a hot cup of your favorite winter beverage in celebration of this season.

Psalm for Candlemas
This psalm may be said as eight candles are lit.
Light one candle for the Hebrew children
   walking into Messiah quest.
Light one candle for the unborn children,
   waiting for an understanding "yes."
Light one candle for the poor and the hungry,
   wanting what we have in full.
Light one candle for the sick and the dying,
   watching for eternity's pull.
Light one candle for the weak and the sinful,
   wasting their days with self-love.
Light one candle for the new in our church
   waiting for the descending dove.
Light one candle for the old and the lonely
   wondering lost in the night.

Light one candle for we, who are faithful,
    working to share the Light. Amen.

Vespers on the Feast of Saint Blase (February 3)
Preparation: On the prayer table place a green cloth with a small platter filled with bones (turkey, chicken, or fish), as well as a Christ candle, which is two candles tied in the shape of an X. Choose a peaceful song to play.

Presider: O God, come greet us in the night!
All: Make haste to help us.

Opening Prayer
On this night of holy Blase
Teach us to walk into your healing light.
May this ancient saint give us courage
to ask for unspoken dreams of wholeness.
We ask this in the name of the Christ. Amen.

Scripture
> Therefore lift your drooping hands and strengthen your weak knees, and make straight paths for your feet, so that what is lame may not be put out of joint, but rather be healed.
> Pursue peace with everyone, and the holiness without which no one will see the Lord. See to it that no one fails to obtain the grace of God; that no root of bitterness springs up and causes trouble, and through it many become defiled.
> (Hebrews 12:12–15)

Word of the Lord
Presider: What is it that keeps you from holiness? Like a bone stuck in our throats, obstacles are what keep us from breathing the holy breath of the Spirit. Tonight, we have an opportunity to ask God with the help of Saint Blase to heal both our bodies and our Spirits. Blase was an ancient saint who interceded for a boy choking on a fish bone.

He is willing to intercede for all those who have come after that small child with the same faith.

Prayer

O God, just like a bone stuck in my throat
are all those things that
keep me from you.
The bone of guilt
that says I can never make up for my failures.
The bone of unforgiveness,
that says no one could love me if they knew what I did.
The bone of bitterness,
that says I will not let go of my grudge.
The bone of hatred
that says I will never reach out to the despised one.
Take away the bone that causes me to choke and die.
Let your marvelous touch free me from death,
Through the intercession of Saint Blase.

Ritual

Presider: We invite you to take one of the small bones on our prayer table. As you hold it allow the Holy Spirit to reveal to you what area of your life is in need of God's healing touch. Perhaps it is a lack of self-esteem, resentment for an act of hatred against you, or anger over an injustice. Whatever comes to your mind, see it in the bone.

You are invited to come forward now and receive the ancient blessing of Saint Blase. As the words of blessing are pronounced, spiritually release the bone stuck in your spirit. Ask God to make you whole in mind and body.

After receiving the blessing, place the bone around the Christ candle as a symbol of your willingness to let go and breathe deep the grace of healing. *Play quiet music during the blessing. As participants come forward, say the following blessing as the Saint Blase candles are placed in front of the throat.*

Through the intercession of Saint Blase, bishop and martyr, may God deliver you from all illness, diseases of the throat, and whatever keeps you from wholeness and holiness. Amen.

Closing Prayer

Glory be to the Father,
who yearns for our wholeness.
Glory be to the Son,
who loves us eternally.
Glory be to the Holy Spirit,
who dreams with us about the days to come.
Amen.

Blessing Before Sending Valentines
In the days before this traditional love note feast, purchase or make some cards. Then separate the envelopes and ask the Holy Spirit to inspire you with the names of those who have loved you in a special way in the last year. Write their names on the envelopes and put a love message on each card before you tuck it into the envelope. Then say the following prayer.

May these messages of love
bring a little red grace
to those who have loved me, Lord.
This little
red grace
is meant to lie
gentle on their
hearts,
meant to warm their soul
with the soft touch
of your divine love.
This little red grace
comes like a whisper

a sweet nothing,
that speaks of a
hundred times
when they said
yes,
yes,
yes,
to loving me.
O most compassionate God,
do not let these
acts of love
go unnoticed
return this love
with your Love
and hold them
in the palm of your hand. Amen.

Connection: Read Matthew 5:43–48. Send an additional Valentine to that one person you find most difficult to love.

The Chair of Peter (February 22)

Jesus the carpenter,
on the feast of the holy chair,
you remind us
to look closely at the things around us,
because things are not really what they seem.
O Jesus,
while a chair
is a just a chair,
this ancient throne
becomes the sign
of your enduring presence

through the line of shepherds.
How many chairs did you learn to make
in the company of father Joseph?
The throne of Peter
becomes a memory of you,
humble carpenter,
maker of chairs,
pope to pope,
the chair continues
and what is so wonderful
is that the seat
proclaims your faithful care.
In the sitting
of each keeper
of the keys.
Jesus,
bless them all,
and keep this ancient church
alive with your presence
through the men who sit upon the chair of Peter.
Amen.

Leap Year Day Prayer (F, S)

When you are given this extra day, plan something unique that you will remember for years. Do something you've never done before—eat a foreign dish, visit a new place, learn a new skill.

In the classroom you can make a leap year time capsule. Fill a shoe box with things that describe life at the school, church, community. Include the price of a loaf of bread, popular movies and songs—whatever you want to remember about this time. Keep the box until the next leap year day, when you can open it with another class and show them how much has changed in four years.

Lent

In our Christian tradition, Lent is a time to get rid of our junk, a kind of spiritual, psychological, and physical housecleaning. As spring looms on the horizon, everyone is energized by a shift in the weather to longer, warmer days. This energy forces us to abandon our tired winter ways to make room for new life. The season frames the church's journey through Lent to Easter well and serves to call each of us into the mystery of transformation in Christ.

Family life moves with the seasons, too. Children are bored with winter activities. Parents are equally bored with such comments as, "I have nothing to do," and "Mom, make him stop looking at me!"—all of which stem from having nothing better to do than stir up a little excitement. Winter confinement forces the whole family to be a little too familiar with its own good and bad habits. The family, as the domestic version of the church, faces Lent as a time to open the windows of our hearts, minds, and bodies to the potential for new beginnings, the grace of rebirth. This dynamic offers a new energy that can make these forty days not a begrudging "giving up" period, but a season of rejuvenating our tired spirits.

In the classroom, life can become mundane as schedules develop into patterns. Even the best teachers are challenged to keep learning interesting when students become bored with these patterns. Lent and the whispers of spring invite us to think in new ways and open mental and spiritual windows for a little of the Holy Spirit's fresh air. Lent challenges us to change and grow into more than we thought we could be. The tempo of life begins to speed up as both students and teachers stretch their souls toward new potential.

Families and classrooms can jog their lenten spirits into the mood of the season by simple signs and practices. These activities provide tangible expressions that keep our lenten efforts in perspective. They encourage creativity in emptying ourselves for God.

Mardi Gras Meal Prayer and Ritual
Preparation: Put purple, green, and gold fabric on a table. Fill the table with the festive food of Mardi Gras. Cue music for the hymn "When the Saints Go Marching In." Place six candles at center of the table. Cover the table in Mardi Gras beads.

Opening Hymn: "When the Saints Go Marching In"
While the song is sung everyone stands and processes in a lively fashion around the table. Continue to march around the table until the last word is sung. At the end of the music remain in place at the table.

Leader: Let us rejoice in the last hours before the holy season of Lent begins.
All: Thanks be to God!
First Reading: Joel 2:12–18
Psalm Prayer: Psalm 121
Side One: I lift up my eyes to the mountain: From where shall come my help? My help shall come from the Lord who made heaven and earth.
Side Two: May God never allow you to stumble! Let God sleep not, your guard. Neither sleeping nor slumbering, Israel's guard.
Side One: The Lord is your guard and your shade and at your right side stands. By day the sun shall not smite you, nor the moon in the night.
Side Two: The Lord will guard you from evil. God will guard your soul. The Lord will guard your coming and your going, both now and forever.
All: Glory to the Father, and to the Son, and to the Holy Spirit.
As it was in the beginning, is now, and will be forever. Amen.
Gospel: Mark 14:1–9
As each intercession is read, a candle on the table is lit.
Leader: May the weeks of Lent bring us to greater faith and love for Christ. And so we pray:

Response: "Change our hearts this time, O God."

Reader: May we learn the grace of silence and prayer in the days to come, we pray to the Lord...*response.*

May we put aside those things that keep us from you, we pray to the Lord...*response.*

May we fast with new energy and understanding in these lenten days, we pray to the Lord...*response.*

May we put aside all worldly distractions and choose to go into the desert with Jesus, we pray to the Lord...*response.*

May we receive the Eucharist often during these holy days, we pray to the Lord...*response.*

May we share our wealth with greater generosity in the weeks ahead, we pray to the Lord...*response.*

Leader: These six weeks of Lent lie before us as an invitation to holiness. May they be like bright beacons leading us to Easter...*response.*

Ritual: Wearing the Beads of Mardi Gras

Leader: On our table we have a gift for each of you. The traditional Mardi Gras beads are waiting to be received. These beads are the sign of Fat Tuesday. They are meant to remind us that this is a night of joyful noise before the silence of repentance arrives. Let the beads stay with you during your Lent as a reminder that if you are faithful to the lenten discipline your Easter joy will be so much more intense than the shallow joy of earthly pleasure.

As you take a necklace from the table, silently name the one area of your life in which you pray for renewal and change. As you place the beads around your neck commit yourself to that change. After this night, place the beads some place where you will see them each day to renew your commitment to this change.

Invite everyone to take a necklace and play again in the background "When the Saints Go Marching In."

Blessing of the Food

Leader: Now we go to the feast of our table with hearts full of gratitude, let us pray:

God of our sustenance,

bless this banquet.

Let it be a reminder of your bountiful love.

May this meal be spiritual nourishment for the long fast of Lent.

Let our communion and care for one another

at this table give us joy and strength

as we await your Easter grace.

Amen.

Let us go now to enjoy the ancient alleluia and celebrate this night.

All: Thanks be to God.

Closing Hymn: "Alleluia"

Prayer to Get Ready for Lent

God of Mercy,

I can see the purple coming up on the horizon

like a morning sunrise

predicting a storm.

It is the early warning of the time of rebirth.

Lent looms like a spring rain.

I can smell it in the air.

My soul waits quietly

for the onset of the change—

winter death into spring hope.

But, you, O Holy Season Maker,

are not content with the warning signs alone.

It is my soul that you want to provoke

into a willingness to

receive your purple grace.

Where will you take me?

Lent Rain comes to cleanse my heart

of the dirt and filth of another year
of the journey.
"Create a clean heart in me, O Lord."
In these days before the Lent rain
prepare my ears to hear your words
of direction and correction.
Soften my sprit so that the rain
may fall deep into my heart. Amen.

Connection: Fashion a small purple heart out of paper. Write
on it those areas of your life where a clean sweep is needed.
Pray about what you will do during Lent to make changes in
your life that will move you toward God.

Marking Ash Wednesday (F)

The season of Lent starts on Ash Wednesday. This day marks the for-
tieth weekday before Easter Sunday. The day takes its name from the
custom of Christians marking their foreheads with ashes in the form
of a cross. This striking symbol is a visible sign of the beginning of an
inward change of heart. Take your family to the Ash Wednesday
liturgy and wear the ancient ashen cross. On this first day of the forty,
let your outward pride fade into the humility of wearing the cross of
those who seek forgiveness. The following is an Ash Wednesday ritual
prayer service you can do at home or school.

Ash Wednesday Gathering Prayer

*Preparation: Put a purple cloth on the prayer table. Remove the Christ
candle and replace it with a large glass bowl of ashes, a bell or chime,
and a CD player with seasonal music.*

Opening Prayer

*A bell or chime is rung one time. Let the sound resolve before the prayer
begins.*

Ancient Holy God, you call us again into the solemn season of Lent. May the sound of this chime cause us to pause and turn round to your lenten grace. Allow the ashes of this Wednesday feast to mark our hearts with the desire to rediscover the ways of discipleship.

Psalm 18:2–4, 7, 47

Leader: Behold! Now is the acceptable time!

All: Now is the day of salvation

Side One: My God I turn to you! My rock, my shield, my champion, my defense.

Side Two: When I call for help I am safe from my enemies.

Side One: From the depths I cry out, my plea reaches the heavens. God heard me.

Side Two: The Lord lives! Blessed be my rock, the God who saves me.

Leader: I love you, God my strength,

All: My rock, my shelter, my stronghold! Glory be to the Father, and to the Son, and to the Holy Spirit. As it was in the beginning, is now, and will be forever. Amen.

Meditation Prayer

The song of ashes
seems as pronounced
as the single
note of a bell.
God invites us into the mystery
of death,
becoming unbelievable birth.
"Come into my sacred heart
and meet my compassionate voice."
O Christ,
from what are we dying?
Into what are we birthing?
The questions ring
in the solemn clang

of the lenten bells.
Something of the sound
reveals his love
telling us to abandon fear
and enter the place where
the questions of the heart are resolved.
The song of ashes
is at once frightening and inviting.
We have no choice
but to respond
and begin, once again,
the marvelous walk into life.

Ritual

Leader: The ashes are an ancient sign that reminds us we were dust and will return to dust. Yet, even in the midst of the frailty of life we are full of hope, because Jesus Christ has claimed us in the waters of our baptism.

As you receive the bowl of ashes take a moment to feel the texture, see the black. Then say quietly, "Lord have mercy" and pass them on.

Pass the bowl of ashes to all present. Give each person a moment to feel the ashes and say the words, "Lord, have mercy." In the background play some reflective seasonal music.

Closing

As the music continues all are invited to share some gesture of peace.

Leader: Let us go now into the season of Lent. May we open our lives to the questions of the heart and the song of ashes. Amen.

Connection: Give each participant a small portion of ashes to keep as a reminder of their lenten walk.

Making a Real Easter Basket (F, S)

On Ash Wednesday, place a shallow tray filled with potting soil in a plastic-lined basket. Plant grass seed in the basket. Put this basket on the dinner table or classroom windowsill. Throughout Lent, watch the grass begin to grow and reflect together on the journey from death to new life. Watch the barren soil spring to life in a lush green carpet. This real Easter basket can be the centerpiece of the Easter table.

Creating Little Blooms to Easter (F, S)

A flower chart helps young children mark lenten days. As each day of Lent passes, or with each good deed or experience, they can add a paper flower or a flower sticker and watch their Lent bloom. Use a large calendar or make a chart for the six weeks of Lent.

Honoring Family Mealtime (F)

Make family meals a special concern during Lent. Lenten meals need not be occasions for austerity. Families can use this time to learn to eat more wisely and simply. Mealtime provides an opportune time for family members to share the happenings of the day in quiet leisure with one another. Our shared experience is another form of nourishment, feeding our hearts and spirits.

Look at the amount of time you spend at the table. Does this time compete with television or other activities? Do you tend to use this time as a forum for correction or criticism? If quality mealtimes are a problem for you, begin this Lent by designating one day a week to gather the whole family for dinner. Serve a simple meal everyone enjoys. Then take the time to listen and interact with one another in an affirming and caring way.

Begin this family meal with a shared prayer. Each week of Lent a different family member could be in charge of the prayer before the meal. Encourage younger children to add to these prayers by asking questions such as: "What good thing happened to you this week that you would like to thank God for?" or "What smells so good on our table? Would you like to thank God for that smell?"

Lenten Prayer Corner (F, S)

Make a family prayer corner somewhere in the house. Find a quiet spot for peace and recollection. Perhaps you can put a comfortable chair near a sunny window with a small table next to it. Place the Scriptures and lenten readings there. Put a small crucifix on the table. Encourage family members to spend a little time there each day. Don't forget to enjoy the luxury of this place yourself.

The classroom, too, should have a permanent prayer corner that children use throughout the year. During Lent, extend this corner by creating a place where students can quietly read spiritual books and the Bible. Each day, display the daily readings from the liturgy or a short verse from Scripture in this corner. Put a crucifix on the wall in this area and place a small Easter basket beneath the cross with a pencil and paper next to it. Invite students to write special prayer requests and place them in the basket. At the end of each week, pray together using the papers in the basket.

Displaying the Cross (F, S)

Make a simple cross from two branches or hang a store-bought cross on a prominent wall in your home or classroom. Add the inscription: "If you love me, take up your cross and follow me."

If you have an outdoor display area, erect a large cross in the schoolyard during Holy Week. This cross can be used in an outdoor Way of the Cross service.

Wearing the Cross (F, S)

For centuries Christians have worn simple crosses to remind them of their discipleship. Use this time to encourage your family or students to wear a cross or crucifix (a crucifix is a cross with the figure of Christ on it). Simple wooden crosses can be purchased inexpensively. You might like to distribute these to your family or students when you make commitments to perform lenten resolutions. The cross gently reminds us to keep the disciplines of the season.

Contributing to a Poor Box (F)

Establish a poor box for the season. Every time you save money by buying lesser cuts of meat, eating a meatless meal, eating at home rather than at a restaurant, choosing not to rent a video or see a movie, walking instead of driving—whatever you can do to save a little bit— put the savings in your box. On Good Friday empty the box and donate the money to your favorite charity.

Examining Your Conscience Together (F)

Forgive someone against whom you hold a grudge, and encourage your children to do the same. Hold a simple evening prayer time to call to mind the need to forgive in our lives. Share ways in which you would like forgiveness in your household. If you have noticed some hurtful or unloving actions during the week, bring them up at this time. Close the prayer time by reading Colossians 3:12–13.

Writing on the Rock (F, S)

The entrance to the tomb of Jesus was closed with a huge rock. This rock was so large that when the women came to the tomb they thought they would need help moving it. We all have hard places in our hearts and lives that keep us from meeting the Savior. These rocks prevent us from loving one another. To develop this idea, put a large rock and a permanent felt pen in the center of the table or in your prayer corner. Encourage family members or students to write on the rock the things that keep them away from growing in their relationship with Jesus. Young children might write, "fighting with my brother," or, "not doing my homework," while teenagers might sneak up to the rock to write, "worrying too much about grades." Moms and dads might write about spending more time listening to their children. Let the rock fill up with this reconciling graffiti during Lent and watch the hard places in your hearts disappear.

The Sacrament of Reconciliation

Prepare your family to participate in your parish reconciliation service. Support your parish community in this liturgical event. Your participation speaks loud and clear to your children of your belief in the sacramental life of our church.

In the classroom spend extra time reviewing the importance of the sacrament of reconciliation. Design invitations for students' families from the Good Shepherd, who personally invites them to the parish reconciliation service.

Proclaiming a Fast (F)

Fast and abstain from more than food this Lent. Discuss with the family some common bad habits. Look at what positive steps you can take together to change unhealthy ways. Resolve to listen more attentively to your spouse, work as a family at picking up messy rooms, attempt to limit the house noise of radios, phones, and television. Resolve to cut down on the amount of driving and use of gasoline.

This attempt at fasting is not for God's benefit. We need it to put our family life in a more loving perspective. It is not so much that we deny ourselves as it is an attempt to seek a more life-giving way to live in God's presence.

Making a Paschal Candle (F, S)

Make your own paschal candle. Decorate a large candle with Easter symbols as well as your family name. Light this candle on Holy Saturday night and pray by its light.

For a lenten art project, students can design their own candles for use with their families, adding personal symbols that represent their faith and the joy of Easter. Paper cutouts can be glued to the wax, melted crayons can be used for paint, and colored tissue paper can be decoupaged in place with white glue.

Witnessing a Metamorphosis (F, S)

This is a great opportunity to do a little collaborative learning. Purchase a cocoon kit from a science catalogue or local natural science store. Arrange to begin this project about two weeks before Holy Week. It takes just a few weeks for the butterflies to emerge from their cocoons. As children watch the cocoon become a butterfly share the story of Christ's death and resurrection. Out of the darkness of death comes the hope of new life. For younger students share a children's story based on this theme.

Purple Paper Chain of Love (F, S)

This project came from a grade school in New Orleans, Louisiana. Students there created a chain of purple paper that extended completely around the interior walls of the school hallways. Each week the students added links for each act of love they performed in the previous school week. By the end of Lent the school was literally surrounded by love. This could be a wonderful family project as well. The purple chains could encompass the interior walls of the kitchen or family room.

"Me-Free" Day (F, S)

Invite family members or students to spend a whole day not using the pronouns *me* or *I*. Give each person five safety pins. Tell them to make chains of the pins and attach them to their shirts. If you hear another person using *me* or *I*, you can ask for a pin. The person with the most pins at the end of the day receives a reward. This simple game calls attention to how much time you focus on yourself. Adolescents especially find "Me-Free" Day painful, yet enlightening.

Visiting a Temple (F, S)

Our Christian heritage finds its roots in the Jewish faith. Lent is a perfect time to plan a trip to a local synagogue or temple. You might even plan an exchange program between young students of the temple and those of your church. To understand the Jewish faith gives rich insight into the life of Jesus. Be sure students understand that the Jewish people weren't responsible for the death of Jesus. With older students you might want to discuss the abuses that resulted from such erroneous assumptions in the past. As you prepare to celebrate Holy Thursday look at Jesus' spirituality in light of his Hebrew roots. You might consider celebrating a seder meal in your home.

Sponsor an Impoverished Child (F, S)

Decide as a class or a family to sponsor a child through a Christian mission agency. This project witnesses to the beatitudes in a direct way; it also teaches the joy of helping those in need. Display your child's picture and pray for your child daily. Encourage family members and students to contribute from their own savings to support this distant sister or brother. This project can continue long after the Easter lilies have faded. Keep your lenten hearts throughout the year as you reach out to the developing world's poor.

Beatitudes Bulletin Board (F, S)

This project is useful on a classroom or kitchen wall. Create a bulletin board or poster that features one beatitude each week of Lent (see Matthew 5:3–11 for a list of the beatitudes). Ask students to find pictures or news articles that feature each week's beatitude (for example, "Blessed are those who mourn"). At the end of each day, pray for the people added to the display. This simple project brings the awareness of human suffering into focus and offers a view of the world that keeps the message of the gospel alive in our daily lives.

Dying to the Self (F, S)

All of us need to understand what it means to "die to the self." This project brings the meaning home and helps gardeners get ready for their spring planting. Prepare planting trays with potting soil. Put flower or vegetable seeds in a small basket next to the soil. Make a sign with the quote, "Very truly, I tell you, unless a grain of wheat falls into the earth and dies, it remains just a single grain; but if it dies, it bears much fruit" (John 12:24).

Every time family members or students do a selfless act of kindness, they can plant a seed. The new seedlings can be transplanted into the garden during the Easter season as living reminders of Jesus' words. Use seeds that are easy to grow and adapt well to transplanting (marigold, impatiens).

MARCH

It is the month of lambs and lions! We begin in the quiet of winter's late slumber, while inklings of life begin to appear on the earth. The wind picks up as first sprouts poke through the ground. Snow and ice, sun and rain, cold and warmth confuse everyone. There is no use predicting what will come. In a wonderful way the earth speaks of mystery in March. The radical change that March brings tells us to let go of our expectations and trust our Creator.

These days are also filled with penance, fasting, reconciliation, and lenten prayer. Christ's passion and death come to us as story, ritual, and mystery once again. March is the backdrop for our ancient redemption story. This story requires a presence a, a mindfulness that is comfortable with the stillness that March provides.

Flying a Kite (F, S)

This windy month is a perfect time to fly a kite. You can invite children and their parents to a kite-flying contest. Ask each child-parent group to design and build a kite. The first Saturday in March, gather everyone at an open field to see whose creation can fly the longest and highest. Be sure to award the winners. Follow this fun with a brown-bag lunch.

Michelangelo's Birthday (March 6) (F, S)

This Renaissance artist left a legacy of wonderful paintings, sculptures, and architecture. To celebrate his genius, hold a birthday party for him. Decorate with pictures of his paintings and buildings. Serve Italian food. Ask each person to mention a favorite work by Michelangelo and why it's a favorite. Get out an art history book and play a game of Renaissance art trivia.

First Day of Spring (March 20) (F, S)

Celebrate the spring equinox by putting fresh flowers in your house or classroom. Put a sweetheart rose on a friend's desk with a note that says, "Happy Spring." Arrange a vase of daisies on the kitchen table. Start a compost pile for future flowers. Let the blooms proclaim that spring has sprung!

Use the first day of spring as an excuse to go for a walk. Most Americans typically spend most of their day indoors. Get out! Walk around the block, listen to the sounds of life around you, stare at the trees, the sky, the water, and the sand. When you return, read Psalm 104.

Another first-day-of-spring project is to build a home for the birds. You can purchase a kit in a nature store or craft shop, or build one from found materials. Hang it in a quiet spot and watch some parents-to-be set up spring housekeeping in your creation.

Gutenberg Bible (March 22) (S)

This is the day the first printed Bible appeared. To celebrate this historic event ask students to bring their family Bible to class. Ask everyone to pick a favorite verse from the Bible and memorize it. Have a Bible Bee: Read the first part of familiar lines from Scripture. Ask contestants to complete the line or phrase. The last one standing wins.

Saints and Heroes

March 3 • Saint Katharine Drexel (F, S)

Saint Katharine Drexel was born in Philadelphia in 1858 to an affluent banker and his wife. Katharine's parents raised her to believe that their wealth was just on loan and was meant to be shared with the less fortunate. When they took Katharine and their other children from Philadelphia to visit the West, Katharine was transformed after witnessing the poverty among Native Americans. Eventually, Katharine gave up all she had to become a sister of the Blessed Sacrament. Over the course of her life, she opened sixty schools for Native and African Americans throughout the southwest and western United States. Pray to her today for all those who still suffer from poverty and injustice throughout the world.

March 8 • Saint John of God (F, S)

This saint founded a religious order dedicated to caring for the sick. To celebrate the feast, invite a health-care professional to the classroom and let students interview this person. Ask the person to share with the class the ways in which this work is ministry.

Take time out to write to your favorite nurses, doctors, nursing home workers, or parishioners who visit the sick. Tell them how much they are appreciated. Thank them for their generous spirits. Pray and fast for these dedicated ministers on this day.

March 10 • Harriet Tubman (F, S)

Nicknamed "Moses," Harriet Tubman helped more than three hundred fellow slaves escape to freedom through the Underground Railroad system. Born in captivity in Maryland and then treated cruelly her entire youth by her owners (and then by her own husband, who threatened to turn her in if she attempted escape), Tubman lived a life that would make most of us shudder in horror. Yet, despite all the obstacles and abuse she faced, she was determined to help others. After her own escape to the North, she served in the Civil War for the Union as a cook and a spy, and went on to be a leading abolitionist. Renowned the world over for her work to bring justice to slaves, she did not stop there. Before her death she worked tirelessly for the suffragist movement, to bring justice and rights to women as well. Throughout it all, Tubman could not read or write. But with the help of a friend, she tackled this obstacle as well and narrated her own autobiography. Tubman's is the face of resilience, peace, and understanding—all of the best qualities a person can possess. Pray today to be more like her. Pray that you, too, can stand up to injustice, overcome obstacles and abuse, and help bring understanding to others.

March 16 • Saint Sarah (F, S)

Sarah, the wife of Abraham, became a mother in her old age and is the grandmother of Judaism, Islam, and Christianity. The story of Sarah teaches us that nothing is impossible with God. Sarah's great charism was that she had enough faith to go with the flow.

On Sarah's feast spend time with your grandmother. Visit her, write her a letter. If she is deceased, visit her grave or light a candle in her honor. In the home or in the classroom, share stories from your grandmothers' lives that enriched your own faith. Invite a grandmother to share her life story with you on this day if your own grandmother cannot be with you.

March 17 • Saint Patrick (F, S)

Legend tells us Patrick introduced the Easter fire to the church. Fire symbolizes the fire of God's love and Christ as our light. On this night build a fire in your fireplace or go to a park and build an outdoor fire. As you watch the flames share the story of Saint Patrick and invite everyone to join you at the Easter Vigil service as the church proclaims, "Christ our Light."

If you have small children hide a little "pot of gold" in lunch bags on this Irish feast. Put chocolate gold coins in a napkin in the bag along with a green cookie. Be sure to include a little note.

March 19 • Saint Joseph (F, S)

Celebrate Joseph as the father of Jesus. In Italy this day is the occasion for extravagant meals. A plate is set at the table for Saint Joseph and it is filled with food. After the meal, the extras are taken to the hungry and poor. This practice of giving food to the poor in honor of Joseph could become a canned food project. On March 19 ask everyone in your school to bring canned foods to the statue of Saint Joseph or a large container labeled the "Joseph Pot." Take this offering to a local food pantry.

As a family, prepare a meal for someone who is sick or unemployed. Deliver it with a "Happy Saint Joseph Day" card and your best wishes and prayers.

In the school celebrate the feast of Saint Joseph with a special morning liturgy. Invite all the fathers of the school and parish. After the liturgy, invite the dads to the classrooms for a breakfast of juice and donuts. When students return home that evening, remind them to honor Dad with a special treat or act of kindness.

March 25 • Mary, on the Feast of Her Annunciation (F, S)

This is "Hail Mary" day. Pray the words of this ancient prayer with a reflective pause after each line. Gather your family or class together and say this prayer with new meaning on the day Mary agreed to become the Mother of God.

This is the day Mary said yes to God. Ask your students how they are asked to say yes to God. Have them each write the word *YES* on one side of a piece of paper. On the other side, have the children write some ways they are called to live out this yes. Advise them to carry this note in their pocket all day.

Another activity for the classroom, is to make YES buttons in honor of Mary, who said yes when asked to become the Mother of God. Ask students to wear the buttons all day. Encourage them to share the meaning of their buttons with anyone who asks. The next day, have students share the moments when they were asked what the button meant.

Another activity for both at home and school is to listen to Schubert's or Gounod's beautiful musical version of the *Ave Maria*. Listen to the music with a sense of prayerfulness. This occasion presents an excellent opportunity to explain the Latin words to our children. This ancient language is part of our Catholic heritage, yet the post–Vatican II generation has little understanding of its meaning.

Prayers
World Day of Prayer Service for All Christians (First Friday in March)
Preparation: Set up a circle of candles (enough candles for each church in your community) with a cross in the middle on a table. Place a basket of cards with the names of your community churches on the table next to the cross.

Invocation
Leader: Let us gather in name of God is moves among us with wondrous mystery. Come into this circle of prayer all you who love him and know that we are one in his spirit. Let us begin with a joyful noise!
Opening Hymn: "We Gather Together"
Make a list of the names of the Christian churches in your community. Pick a card from the basket. Insert the name of each church in the following litany. As each church is mentioned a candle is lit.
Reader: For the people of God at _____,
may they prosper and grow in faith.

After all the churches have been mentioned, say the following prayer.
All: God of us all, we lift up to you the many-faceted beauty of the churches gathered here. You give us each the power of your word, the wonder of the faith walk and the hope of the life to come. Blend us into a marvelous tapestry of grace. Renew our determination to reach out to one another in service and love.

Ritual of Peace
Leader: Reach out to those around you in a gesture of goodwill. With a handshake or hug, share God's love among us. (Now, the gathering exchanges some token of love while the closing hymn is played quietly). As we leave this gathering, please take a card on which you will find the name of one of our community churches. We ask that on this Friday you offer up a fast for this church. Perhaps you could abstain from meat, or turn off the car radio. Whatever little act of fasting you

could send to God to express your desire for unity and concern for the church on the card you have chosen.

Closing Hymn: "He's Got the Whole World in His Hands." *Insert the names of the churches in each verse.*

Saint Katharine Drexel (March 3)
Holy Katharine,
visionary of a thousand faces,
smiling into the sun,
smiling into the Son.
Your legacy stands
as a triumphant victory
over discrimination
and ignorance.
May we be granted your vision,
and your heart.
May we,
in union with you,
never believe
that anyone
cannot fulfill
God's dream.
Never believe
that who we are
limits
God's vision.
Never believe
that God's sacred promises
are meant for only
a few. Amen.

*Prayer for Understanding to Commemorate Harriet Tubman
(March 10)*
God the Image Maker,
remake my heart
into a heart
like good Harriet.
She saw others
with unwavering kindness.
Let me see everyone
with kindness in mind.
She believed in justice
and the goodness of human beings.
Let me stand up
for fairness.
As a natural reflex,
she would not let evil
overcome good.
Let me work to overcome darkness,
No matter what the cost.
Amen.

Morning Psalm on the Ides of March (March 15)
Ancient feast of ides,
meets us with the dawn!
But no longer are we transfixed
in its waking.
Caesar's most unlucky day
gives us a moment to embrace
the victor over death and luck.
Jesus,
we greet you
with sure confidence.
You conquered the fear of death

and disaster.
By your death and rising
teach us to regard
magic and luck
as worthless trinkets
in the hands of those
who do not know your story.
Teach us to stand
firmly in grace.
Teach us to
turn this unlucky day
into the day of salvation. Amen.

Connection: The Ides of March was regarded in ancient times as the unluckiest day of the year. Superstitions like this have no place in the life of a disciple. What little superstitions do you hang on to? Make a list of things or actions you consider unlucky. Throw the list away and promise yourself never to be tempted to practice these superstitions again.

A Single Mother's Prayer to Saint Joseph (March 19)
Saint Joseph,
man of virtue and justice.
Tzaddik
is Hebrew word
for a man such as you.
A just man, says Matthew,
and yet you are so much more.
You are the guardian
of the virgin and child,
the keeper of the house,
the secure gate,

the fire maker through the dark night.
As you kept your wife and child safe,
keep us safe, too.
In the stark loneliness of my home
be a holy guardian.
Show me the way.
Stay here as a spiritual presence,
keeping our little family safe
and close to God. Amen.

Connection: In the tradition of Sicily, create a Saint Joseph's table, a buffet supper to share with the poor. Since Saint Joseph's feast occurs during Lent, plan to host a meal for a single mom and her children, or a poor family as a form of almsgiving. If you are not up to the feast, plan to volunteer at a soup kitchen on March 19 in honor of good Saint Joseph.

Psalm of the Vernal Equinox
We see the lengthening of days
as the earth's only way
of showing light, Blessed Light!
Light!
Light in abundance
for all those who believe!
Equal night and days
surround us in this holy pause.
Lent puts down her purple banner
just long enough
for us to notice
hope
on the horizon.

It is in this mystical dawn
that we see once again
the ancient promise
that the night of sin
will never
outlast the
Day of Love. Amen.

Connection: On these two days in late March (21–22) pause to
watch the sun rise and set. Take stock of your lenten progress.
Make a list of what you can do in the rest of Lent to bring
Easter sunrise joy into your soul.

Prayer for the Feast of the Annunciation (March 25)
My soul
magnifies
and praises God
in all places.
My spirit rejoices with Mother Mary,
because through her
God continues to do
great things.
God continues to bless all women
because of the courage
of Holy Mary's
quiet *fiat*
Her YES
is our yes.
We offer God
all that we are
believing that
God flushes our spirits

with grace.
And we like
our mother
can do
whatever he asks. Amen.

Connection: What is God asking you to say yes to in your life? What quiet hope, impossible dream, do you keep deep within? Write the word YES on a piece of paper. On the other side write a statement of your dream. Now, spend some time with Mother Mary, and pray for her help in saying yes to your dream and God's dream for you.

Mid-Lent Morning Prayer Ritual
Preparation: Place a piece of purple cloth, a cross, a twig, and a bowl with incense on the prayer table. Place a small piece of purple ribbon for each participant around the incense bowl. Have a CD player ready to play reflective music.

Opening Prayer
Father of mercy, we await your forgiveness. As sure as the sun has risen this day, spreading pink-purple light across the darkness, so your grace will enter the darkest places of our souls. It is not enough to wait upon your mercy. We will walk in the purple grace you offer with certain hearts that you listen to us and forgive.

Scripture: Psalm 86

Meditation
Purple falls gently on the soul
that is willing to let her fall.
She cannot distinguish between
sinner

and mystic.
She only knows the
Incarnate Lover approaches.
Purple mounts the days into Triduum
with determined grandeur,
for God is greater than our most hidden
fear.
She lies gently upon us
surrounding our shoulders
with her mantle of mercy
and we are won
not so much by guilt
but by love. Amen.

Ritual

Light a bowl of incense and play some reflective music in the background.

Leader: As incense rises, so do our prayers before God. What is the one area of your life that you would most like to change? Perhaps an area of failure that plagues you or a pattern of behavior that you cannot escape? Imagine that this need for change is rising to God in the holy incense. See it going toward the heart of God. Believe that God understands your need. (Pause.) When you are ready, come forward and take a small piece of purple ribbon. Allow this splash of purple to remind you of the grace of the second half of Lent. Now, is the time to deal with your impossible obstacle to wholeness and holiness. Resolve to change that pattern that produced your failure. (Pause.) Think of one thing you can do to begin that change. (Pause.) As you come forward to claim your ribbon resolve to keep it with you until Triduum. Each day do something to make this change in your life. (Participants come forward as the music quietly plays.)

Closing Prayer

God of New Beginnings
and Impossible Hope,
we ask that these ribbons
be for us a sign of happy endings.
May all that hinders us from loving you,
disappear with the sweet incense of our regret.
May your mercy rain down upon
our contrite and hopeful hearts. Amen.

Connection: Journal about the purple ribbon. What obstacle to faith does it represent? What can you do to change? Continue this journal throughout the rest of Lent. Begin to note your little victories over death, day by day.

HOLY WEEK

Holy Week is a time when all the symbols, the drama and energy of our faith come together for one dynamic, faith-filled experience. The liturgies of this week express the very identity of our discipleship. In our families and classrooms we should revel in the gospel stories of Jesus' passion, death, and resurrection, because in these stories we find the seeds of faith. Children and adults need to smell the chrism oil, break the bread, watch the vigil fire, and play in the waters of baptism. It is a week to touch the symbols and soak up the wonder of the paschal mystery. The following activities encourage the child in all of us to live and experience Holy Week.

Monday (F)
This is the day to make your plans for the week. Plan to attend your parish liturgies as a family. Get babysitters for your preschoolers, plan easy meals so that you are ready to get out the door in time for the evening services. The effort will seem too great without a little preplanning. Let your family know ahead of time the "what and when" of these family times.

Decorating the Easter Tree (F, S)
Spray paint a small twiggy branch white. Then ask your young children to make caterpillars by rolling pipe cleaners around pencils. Hang the caterpillars on the tree. On Holy Saturday remove the caterpillars and replace them with butterflies made from wallpaper scraps, bright-colored magazine pictures, or construction paper and crayons. Add bits of colored tissue paper as flowers. The butterflies remind us of our new life in Jesus. On Easter you can add colored eggs and other symbols to your tree.

Buying New Clothes (F, S)

It is a tradition in many families to wear new clothing on Easter as a symbol of our new life through the Resurrection. An "Easter outfit" should mean more than being the best-dressed in the Easter parade! Plan ahead and purchase one new item for each member of your family. Whether it's a new tie for dad or a hat for little daughter, let everyone "put on Christ" in new garments.

Tuesday

Prepping a Holy Week Garden (F)

Find a small garden spot outside and plant some spring flowers. Then create a small tomb out of modeling clay and set a big rock next to the tomb. On Friday add three small wooden crosses. On Saturday put the rock in front of the tomb. On Easter morning roll away the rock, remove the crosses and put a piece of white cloth in the tomb. Read the appropriate sections of the passion story as you make these changes in your Holy Week garden.

Delivering a Secret Basket (F, S)

Purchase an empty Easter basket and fill the bottom with plastic grass (or shredded paper from the office). Ask everyone to add items to the basket throughout the week. On Easter Sunday deliver the basket to someone who is lonely and needs this joyful treat.

This gift basket is a great outreach project for the classroom. Ask each student to bring in one item for the basket. On the last day of school, ask a volunteer parent to deliver the basket to a homebound parishioner. If possible, take this person's photograph with the basket. Share the photo with the class upon their return to school.

Wednesday

Distributing the Chrism Oils (F)

This is the day the holy oils are distributed to churches for use in the rites throughout the liturgical year. If possible, attend the Chrism Mass celebrated in your diocese. The diocesan newspaper or parish bulletin will have the date, time, and place for this liturgy at which the oils are blessed.

At your evening meal on this night, bless a small bottle of oil. You might want to use bath oil or essential oil from a specialty store that sells crafts supplies, candles, and potpourri. Use this oil at home in the coming year. The ancient custom of using oil for comfort, healing, and anointing can become a new and meaningful tradition in the domestic church, our homes. On this night after the oil is blessed, ask everyone to anoint each others' forehead with oil in the Sign of the Cross.

Prayer for the Blessing of Oils on Holy Wednesday
Preparation: Fill a cruet with baby oil or some other fragrant oil. Put it on your prayer table.
On this day the church blesses the sacramental oils at the Mass of Chrism. Non-sacramental oil can be used in the Catholic home as a symbol, recalling the action of holy oils. These ordinary oils can be used for prayer when a member of the family is ill, to anoint someone with a special need or just to massage weary feet and hands. While these blessing oils are not meant to duplicate the holy oil of the church, they are a good way to teach the beauty of oil in the Catholic tradition.

Blessing Prayer

Jesus, we remember the day when you allowed the woman to anoint your feet with ordinary oil. We have brought our ordinary oil to you today. Bless it for our use. May you see it as a sign of healing prayer in our lives. We offer you this sign as a gesture of our belief in your healing, soothing power. Teach us to rub it deep into our skin and our spirits. Let it be for us the touch of your compassionate hand through the sickness and pain of this year. Amen.

Ritual

Ask everyone gathered to take a little of the oil and sign the cross on the palm of the person next to them. After the anointing invite every-one to rub the oil vigorously into their skin as a sign of their willingness to allow God to touch them.

Prayer

Let us revisit this oil throughout the year,
whenever we ache to feel your holy touch.
As the bleeding woman stretched
to touch the hem of your garment,
we reach out to touch your presence
with this oil. Amen.

Connection: Keep the cruet of oil in a special place. Use it often for personal or family prayer when you need God's healing touch or encouragement.

Holy Thursday
Cooking the Maundy Meal (F, S)

This is a family meal full of symbols. Prepare a centerpiece of grapes and bread for the Eucharist, a coin purse for Judas, and a lantern for the soldiers in the Garden of Olives. Serve thirteen things to represent the number of guests at the Last Supper. Conclude the meal by reading John 18:1–9.

Good Friday
Proclaiming a Fast (F)

On this solemn day agree as a family to spend the entire day talking quietly to one another and fasting from noise. Turn off radios, TVs, phones, and computers. Live this day in quiet reflection with God. Pray and fast as a family. Rest in the presence of the Lord and hear the voice of the Spirit among yourselves.

Dyeing Red Eggs (F)

Dye some eggs red to recall the legend of the first Easter eggs. The legend tells us that Mary Magdalene went to Pontius Pilate on Easter morning to tell him of the Resurrection. She brought him a gift of eggs. Pilate refused the gift and said he would not believe Jesus had risen unless the eggs turned red. In an instant the eggs turned red and Pilate believed! Eat these eggs on the night of the Easter Vigil.

Preparing Easter Eggs (F)

This is the night to create eggs for the feast. The egg is a symbol of hope in new life and has been a part of Easter menus since AD 700. Here are some ways to get creative with your eggs:

Use plastic eggs to hold little symbols of the feast: a rock (for the tomb), a piece of white cloth (for the shroud), a cross (for Jesus' death). Let children collect the symbols and tell their meaning. Reward anyone who knows all the meanings.

Put Easter promises in real eggs. Pierce the ends of raw eggs and blow out the yolks. Color the eggs. Then write down things you will do with your child: a walk, a trip to the zoo, lunch with grandpa, cleaning grandma's house, making cookies for a neighbor, etc. Roll up the slips of paper and push them inside the eggs. In the classroom, have children make a promise egg for their parents. Crack the eggs on Easter to discover the promises of love. These eggs can be used to decorate an Easter tree. Plastic eggs can also be used.

Holy Saturday
Making Breads (F)

On this "tomb day" make your Easter breads. You might want to make hot cross buns, sweet yeast rolls decorated with an icing cross. These breads are symbolic of Christ's rising and victory over the cross.

Filling Easter Baskets (F)

Fill baskets with alternatives to sugary sweets. Try fruit, cheese, and surprises from the grocery shelves that are usually too expensive for everyday cupboards. Everyone in the house should receive a basket—not just the children. Fill Mom's and Dad's with their favorite coffees, teas, or snack foods. See the grocery aisles as a treasury of Easter surprises for everyone. Top off the basket with a few inedibles such as pencils, crossword puzzle books, puzzles, games, hair ribbons, and so on.

Baking the Paschal Lamb Cake (F)
Use a mold to make a cake in the shape of a lamb. This traditional Easter dessert represents the Paschal Lamb who was slain.

Honoring Godparents' Supper (F)
One of the most inspiring parts of the Holy Saturday liturgy is the baptism of the catechumens. This moving ceremony reminds all of us of our own baptism as we join in repeating our baptismal promises. This season is a great time to host a supper for your godparents and the godparents of your children. If the godparents live far away, send them an Easter card or make a phone call to let them know they are in your thoughts.

Praying for the Catechumens (F, S)
Assign each member of your family or class one of the new members of your parish who will be received into the church this night. Pray and fast for these people all day. Send them notes today expressing your joy over their decision to be a part of your church. In your note, share with the new member why you like being Catholic and what it means to you to be Catholic.

Trimming Trees and Planting Gardens (F)
Some Eastern Rite families traditionally plant their spring gardens on Holy Saturday. This is a good time to trim back the deadwood that has accumulated over the past year. In the evening this wood can be used to build an outdoor Easter fire in celebration of this holy night. If it is too early to plant the spring garden, you might use this day to plan your garden and order seeds from seed catalogs. Let every family member grow a favorite flower or vegetable or try a new exotic vegetable.

Easter
The celebration of Christ's Resurrection is not a one-day event for the church. We savor the feast for fifty days, until the Feast of Pentecost. Keep this in mind as you plan your spring. Each day of the Easter sea-

son can offer some reminder of resurrection. The prayers of our Easter liturgies focus on the great privilege we bear as believers in the Resurrection. Keep the joy of Easter morning in your spirits throughout the season. Do everything you can to promote the Alleluia feeling at home, in church, and in the classroom. Easter is not just a holiday full of bunnies and eggs; it is an attitude of inner joy that stays with us long after the jelly beans are gone.

The earth is returning to life and so is the liturgical year. The paschal mystery is right before our eyes. We see it as the first strains of Alleluia ring through the dawn of Easter and we see it in the spring behavior of plants and animals. These are the mystical days of the paschal mystery that keep us hopeful and keep us believing in something beyond our understanding. The grace of April is the grace of renewal and abundant life. It is to be savored and experienced rather than explained.

Visiting Some New Life (F, S)
Use spring vacation to visit newborn animals. Go to the nearest zoo, petting farm, or pet store and enjoy the babies. This experience brings us back to the simple wonder of creation.

Walking to Emmaus (F, S)
In the quiet of the second Sunday of the Easter season, take a solitary walk. If there is a picturesque spot near your home, go there to enjoy the beauty around you. As you walk imagine that Jesus comes to walk with you. Talk to him about your deepest needs as you walk. Then, listen to the thoughts that come to mind as if Jesus is responding to your words. You might try the Emmaus walk as a group venture. Ask everyone to take a solitary walk, then return to the group and share what happened.

Throwing a "Respect Life" Baby Shower (F, S)
During this season, contact a local center that supports the life of the unborn or a day-care center for children of high school mothers. Ask for a list of gifts needed for these babies. Host a baby shower for the

center in your home or classroom. Serve snacks and play games if you wish. You might invite a local representative of the pro-life movement to share ideas with you.

Rewarding the "Star of the Week" (F)
Each week of the Easter season designate one member of the family to be "star of the week." The "star" gets to ride in the front seat of the car with the driver, choose favorite television programs each evening, and choose the menu for Sunday's supper. You can plan other privileges that fit into your family life: favorite cookies, favorite board games, inviting a friend over to spend the night. The idea of this week is to affirm the unique and special people in your family as a sign of God's love for each of us.

Prayers
Housecleaning Prayer Before Easter
Master of the broom and dust rag,
Maker of bugs and crud,
Keeper of the divine house,
muster up in me the call to clean
this dusty, winter-weary house.
Let us shake the drapes.
Let us sparkle the windows.
Let us move the mud.
All in honor of the Alleluia
that even now begins to rumble
the foundation of this little home.
Give me the holy steam
to leave no corner undone.
Let this day of bringing new life to our home
bring new life to my soul.
May I move with determined grace.
Each wall and rug,
lampshade and tabletop

are little tokens of the holy life we share here
with you!
May this little sanctuary of domestic church
be a welcome place for all those who will come here
to celebrate resurrection and hope.
Give me
oomph and push,
swing and zing,
all in your honor. Amen.

Connection: As you clean your home for the Easter holiday, play hymns and holy songs. Sway with the beat and let this cleaning day be a prayer.

Prayer Service for the Season of Easter
Preparation: Prepare the prayer table with a white cloth and a large white candle or paschal candle.

Opening Prayer

Risen Christ, surround us in your mysterious light. Search out the darkest places of our souls and flood the shadows of doubt and despair with your marvelous presence. We are standing speechless at the empty tomb. Give us the courage to believe what we do not see. Give us the faith to understand that you are not within the tomb. Once and for all the victory has been won and you invite us to walk away from death's door and discover new life.

Hymn: Sing an Alleluia Gospel Acclamation

Meditation

Alleluia again!
The fragrant night is upon us,
where purple mercy and dazzling white light
meet in the darkest shadow of creation.

We are surprised again,
again, and
again.
Blood red passion
turns into amazing Alleluia
and we are surprised
again!
You would think
the battle would become old
but we are like newborns
discovering for the first time
that hope exists.
Everything old
becomes new again,
again, and
again!
We are confronted
by the ancient words
He is not here.
And what are we to believe?
That mystery has
overcome reason?
Light floods the morning
and pierces
our doubting souls
again.

Ritual

Begin this ritual by listening to quiet instrumental music. Let everyone listen for a few moments. Then the leader takes the glass bowl of water and the small evergreen branch.

Reader One: Christ is risen and we are called to rise with him into a new life.

All: Alleluia.

Leader sprinkles water to the left and those touched by the water make the Sign of the Cross.

Reader Two: Christ is risen and we have been chosen to share the story.

All: Alleluia.

Leader sprinkles water to the center and those touched by the water make the Sign of the Cross.

Reader Three: Christ is risen and we will see him again in the community of believers.

All: Alleluia.

Leader sprinkles water to the right and those touched by the water make the Sign of the Cross. Leader returns the bowl to the table.

Reader Four: We have been called to follow the Christ. In his dying and rising we have been marked forever with the waters of salvation. He is no longer entombed but stands among us here. Let us be still and know that he is here.

The music continues for a few more moments while everyone contemplates the presence of Christ among them. After this time the music fades away.

Leader: Let us all say again, Alleluia.

All: Alleluia.

Closing Prayer

Go now, to live Alleluia. Christ is risen, we are rising. Alleluia!

APRIL

The earth is coming to bloom again and we are filled with hope. It is a tested hope, as we have seen the wonder of it all so often. Spring provokes us into giddy delight with the pinks, whites, and yellows of blooms that peek at us. The subtle strains of Alleluia begin. It is as if we have never heard it before. April is a time of rebirth in the deepest sense. Being born again means shedding winter's sleep for life, growth, and light. Out of darkness the earth and every soul sees a victory over death, and we rejoice.

April Fools' Day (April 1)
This is a day for silliness and having fun. Taking time to play is important to our well-being.

Brown-Bag Silliness (S)
For lunch, ask students to pack a lunch that they are willing to trade. Be sure parents know about this ahead of time. Each lunch should contain a sandwich, a piece of fruit, and a snack. In addition, every one should include a note with a riddle on it. Put all the lunches in a pile and have students choose one different from the one they brought. After lunch, ask others your riddle until someone offers the correct answer. Remember to thank your donors for the delicious April Fools' lunches.

Silly Supper (F)
Let everyone prepare one part of the meal. Each contribution to the supper must be a secret, silly surprise. For instance, serve a pitcher of blue lemonade (add food coloring); "smiling applesauce" (make a smiling face with raisins for each serving); Dr. Seuss's "green eggs and ham"; gummy worms in chocolate pudding for

dessert. Many such "silly recipes" can be found in children's cookbooks.

Arbor Day (April 10) (F, S)

In many states Arbor Day is celebrated on this date. *Arbor* is the Latin word for "tree." Support the ecological system by planting a tree. These valuable resources return oxygen to our atmosphere. Plant a tree at home, in a local park, or at school in memory of a loved one who has died. This reminder of someone for whom you grieve stands as a living symbol that life does not end with death. Free trees are often available from government agencies and local forestry offices. If you can find a resource for free trees, let each child plant a tree. In the classroom you might invite a forester to speak to students about the value of trees or discuss the value of the rain forest to our earth.

Yom Hashoa (F, S)

On this Jewish feast, all humanity recalls the agony of the Holocaust. The date varies according to the Jewish calendar; it corresponds to April 10, 1945, the beginning of the Allied liberation of Auschwitz. To honor those who died during the Holocaust, have a three-minute period of silence at noon. Share the story of Anne Frank, or perhaps another story of the Holocaust, with your family or class.

Shavuot (F, S)

Shavuot (Shah-VOO-oat) is a Jewish feast celebrated seven weeks after Passover. The date varies, so check your calendar. It is a harvest festival. Families ate a hearty meal of the spring crops and grains, and always left some grain in the field for the poor. This is a thanksgiving meal in gratitude to God for our rich blessings. In the tradition of Shavuot, prepare a basket of fresh breads or muffins and take it to a local soup kitchen along with a cash donation.

Saints and Heroes

April 5 • Saint Noah (F, S)

Noah is the Old Testament hero of the flood and the patron saint of sailors and boat builders. On his feast day, build a miniature raft from craft sticks or twigs. Give your "ark" a name that reminds us of one of the virtues Noah needed to survive the flood (such as "Hope"). Float your creation in a nearby stream, pond, pool, or even a bathtub. If more than one person makes a raft, have a race.

April 9 • Dietrich Bonhoeffer (F, S)

Dietrich Bonhoeffer is a saintly Lutheran minister who opposed Hitler's regime and Nazi policies. He was not afraid to speak out. He died a martyr on this day in 1945 in a Nazi concentration camp. His writings remain for us today as a testament to preach the gospel even in difficult times. In honor of this courageous holy man, write a letter to the editor of your local newspaper about a moral issue that is dear to your heart.

April 11 • Saint Stanislaus

Saint Stanislaus stood up against a cruel king, Boleslaus II—a nasty man who eventually killed him. Poland still reveres the courage and holiness of this eleventh-century hero. Saint Stanislaus is a great saint to call upon when you must confront someone who is doing wrong. On the feast of Saint Stanislaus, offer a fast for those who fight for justice in our world. Make a list of those living men and women who need your prayers to continue to stand up for what is right.

April 23 • Saint George (F, S)

This saint is known as the slayer of dragons. We all have dragons in our lives, those ugly things that need to be done that we ignore. The more we ignore our dragons, the bigger they get! What are some of the dragons in your life? Cleaning the attic, calling Grandma, or balancing the checkbook? On this feast of the dragonslayer, make a list of three of your biggest dragons. Slay these three monsters today and be on the lookout for future dragons.

April 30 • Walpurgis Night
The Roman martyrology lists this day as Saint Walpurgis's Day. But more recently this day is marked in Europe as the last day of winter. May 1, or May Day, brings the spring. Saint Walpurgis was an English nun known as a healer. For centuries people celebrated her feasts by opening up the windows of their homes and blowing out the stuffy winter air with the first breezes of spring. They would build spring fires to burn all the deadwood in their yards. This day is the time to open windows and hearts to the sweet breath of spring.

April 22 • Earth Day
In 1970 the first Earth Day was celebrated. People throughout the country came together to show their concern for the environment, and to raise awareness of the harm humans are causing it. During the Easter season, Christians celebrate a reverence for life. How appropriate to pray for good old Mother Earth in this holy time.

Prayers
Invocation Before a Confrontation
Good Saint Stanislaus,
be with me now.
I do not have the words or the courage to act.
Yet, I cannot sit still and watch
the wrong continue.
Stand with me
in this moment and guide me.
Join with me in heart and soul
as we implore
the Holy Spirit to fill me with the gift
of courage and wisdom,
gifts that are meant for little ones
who need a mighty sword.
May my words
cut.

May my love for goodness
heal.
And may your passion for right
be my own. Amen.

Prayer for Courage to Speak Out
So many silent lips frame the history of injustice.
O Lord, make us strong in the midst of oppression.
Give us your words of righteousness.
Too many have been lost because no one defended them, and
too many never heard the Word because no one would speak it.
May Holy Dietrich inspire us not count the cost
of the fire in our hearts,
but to speak without reserve
so that justice and righteousness
may flourish in our lives. Amen.

Litany for the Earth
Preparation: You will need candles and a chime for this service.
Prayer: Creator of all that is good, forgive us for any injury we have
caused to this little part of your created world. Give us a deeper appreciation of life and help us to support life in all its stages. On this day
we ask to share in your creative work by returning the earth to its original beauty. Give us the means to live lives of purity and compassion
as we care for the marvelous gift of created life.
Reader: For the air that it may be made pure once again so that all
your creatures may be sustained by it. We pray…
All: God of all creation, hear our prayer. *Candle is lit and chime is rung.*
Reader: For the water that it may become clear and purified, so that
it will quench the thirst of the all that lives. We pray…
All: God of all creation, hear our prayer. *Candle is lit and chime is rung.*
Reader: For the soil that it may be replenished to support the fruits of
the earth. We pray…

All: God of all creation, hear our prayer. *Candle is lit and chime is rung.*
Reader: For the animals that roam the earth that they may be fruitful and multiply. We pray…
All: God of all creation, hear our prayer. *Candle is lit and chime is rung.*
Reader: For the unborn that someday every child will be allowed to live. We pray.
All: God of all creation, hear our prayer. *Candle is lit and chime is rung.*

Closing Prayer
God of life, you have every living cell in your hands. You care for all the earth and us. Give us your compassionate heart so that we might begin the work of restoring the earth to its health and beauty. Amen.

Connection: Make a resolution to adapt one new environmentally friendly habit: recycle, stop using the car air conditioner, use real cups instead of Styrofoam, buy things made of recycled products, use both sides of paper before throwing it away, walk instead of driving, or whatever you can do, begin it today as a living prayer for the earth.

M A Y

May is the month of Mary, spring flowers, First Communions, and all things fresh and lovely. It is a time for long walks in gentle breezes, planting gardens, smelling sweet flowers, and experiencing unpredictable adventures. Medieval Maypoles, Marian processions, and outdoor suppers fill the days with whimsy and teach us God is not all business. May is the moment when God dances with us. Ordinary time turns from the deep pine green of late winter to the pale, yellow-green of sprouts and new grass, and all things fresh.

Pentecost can appear at the end of this month. The wind of the Spirit is always welcome, but Pentecost brings together wind and fire. These two ancient symbols bring a message of passion and power that herald the stirrings of new spiritual energy. It is a time to encounter both wind and fire as a holy anointing.

May Day (May 1) (F, S)

This ancient festival of spring is celebrated with dances, songs, and games. It was originally celebrated to ensure fertility and new life. The Maypole dance symbolized the never-ending circle of life and reproduction. In ancient communities children were given little baskets filled with treats as gifts of gratitude for their presence.

We can enjoy this May feast by doing a little dancing ourselves. Roll up the rug and have a May square dance. Borrow a recording from the library or get together with other families and hire a caller. Spend a spring evening learning this fun country-western dance.

In school, May Day dancing could be a great physical education activity. Each class could learn a different ethnic dance—learn to clog, dance an Irish jig, or perform the tango. At the end of the day, gather the whole school and have the classes perform their new dances for the assembly. As an alternative, you might want to invite a group of ethnic dancers to share their gift with you.

Mary Day (S)

Designate one day in early May as Mary Day in your church and school. Plan a full day of activities honoring her. Some parishes begin with a liturgy focusing on the Mother of God. The rosary is prayed in the afternoon. The day could conclude with evening prayer and a potluck supper. Invite a speaker or view a video on the church's Marian teachings. Whatever you do, make this a day of prayer and learning about Mary's place in our faith.

Circle of Roses (F, S)

The word *rosary* means "a circle of roses." It was intended to convey that each Hail Mary is like a rose and our prayers form a circle of prayers that we offer to heaven. Mary is often pictured with roses at her feet. The use of the rosary developed in the Middle Ages as a substitute for the Liturgy of the Hours for those who could not read. The 150 Hail Marys represented the 150 psalms, and the mysteries of the rosary became simple signposts for the events of the Gospels.

Today, the rosary is a popular devotion. This beautiful ritualized prayer and the use of rosary beads as a method of meditation have an honored place in our tradition. The month of May is a perfect time to introduce this devotion to children. If your children do not have a rosary, it is a great project to make one from a kit available at a religious supply store. Then explain the prayers to them. Pray the rosary at least once during May as a family or as a class. It will leave a lasting memory with everyone.

Wearing the Blue (F, S)

The color blue is traditionally associated with Mary. Pick a special day in May to wear something blue in memory of the Mother of God. Another way to remind ourselves of our kinship with Mary is to wear a small, blue ribbon the entire month. This ribbon can be threaded with a small religious "Mary" medal or other symbol of the Virgin. These blue ribbons make perfect remembrances of the parish's Mary event. Young children love to wear these bows with the tiny medal attached. The little symbol makes honoring Mary very real to primary grade students.

Signing the Magnificat (S)

The Magnificat is Mary's hymn of gratitude and praise (Luke 1:46–55). Mary's absolute trust in God is displayed in her beautiful canticle. To enjoy the power of the Magnificat learn to sign the prayer using sign language (find a book at the public library or invite a signing person to teach you). To further highlight the meaning of the prayer, sing it with the signs. This project is a creative communion meditation for school liturgies, as well as a lesson in the art of signing.

Outdoor Rosary With Mini-Plays (F, S)

You can turn the rosary into a dramatic event by taking the beads outdoors. This exercise can be done as a block rosary or as a school project. Assign each class or family a specific mystery of the rosary. Ask them to create a still scene of living statues to depict the Gospel event. Give each class or family a location along the prayer route for their scene. In a neighborhood, each family could use their front yard for their scene. At school, each class could be assigned a different spot on the church grounds. At home, the family could create small scenes with statues on shelves in various rooms.

The entire group begins together. As you reach the first mystery, those who are in the scene leave the group and portray the mystery. The entire decade is prayed in front of the scene after the mystery is announced. You can add a short meditation before the decade if you wish.

This walking journey of prayer is an active way to pray the rosary, especially for children. This outdoor version is a good way to keep them involved and reverent when stationary versions cause distractions. Another approach is listening to an audio version of the rosary.

This devotion is perfect for long car rides or even with earbuds as you walk for exercise.

Origami Bouquets for Mary (F, S)

Origami is the Japanese art of paper folding. This ancient art form is simple, yet produces beautiful results. During the month of May, make origami flowers for Mary's bouquet. The public library offers ample resources for learning origami. You can use lightweight paper to make roses, lilies, and a variety of flowers that last forever.

In the school each class can learn to fold a different flower. These paper bouquets can be displayed at the foot of Mary's statue during the month of May. This art project is a way to unite art instruction with the liturgical signs of Easter and Marian devotion.

Mother's Day

This commercial occasion to give Mom a card and a gift can become much more than a money-spending event. People feel guilty if they ignore Mom on this day, yet they feel manipulated into buying the cards, perfume, and flowers pushed on this day. Here are some noncommercial giving ideas that say, "I love you," without a price tag.

Memory Box (F, S)

Every Mom receives loads of loving mementos from her children throughout the parenting years: love poems, painted rocks, "I'm sorry" notes, and so on. Make a box in which she can keep these memories. A sturdy cardboard box with a cover will do nicely. Decorate the box with self-adhesive paper, paint, pretty wallpaper, or fabric. Label the box with the words, "Mom's Memory Box."

Recipe Book (F, S)

Ask all the moms of your students to submit a recipe that is her child's favorite. Let the students recopy these recipes with their own reflections on why this selection is their favorite and any special memories of when it was served. Ask each child to include a drawn or written portrait of their mom on the recipe page. Assemble all these gourmet treats in one volume. Make copies of your cookbook and let the students give them to their moms as Mother's Day gifts.

Create a "Mother's Cookbook" for your family. Ask all members of your extended family to submit a favorite recipe that their mother or grandmother created or made often. Compile all the entries in a binder and present this family collection to all the households. Save a few copies as gifts for future brides who will join the family.

The Story of Our Mothers (F, S)

If you have a daughter who is grown or almost grown, you will enjoy creating this legacy for her to treasure. Collect a picture of each of her female ancestors (Mother, Grandmother, Great-Grandmother, and so on). Next to each picture write the words, "This is _____, the mother of _____, the mother of _____" in the style of the Old Testament patriarchs. Write a little story about each woman. Tell about her life and times; tell about her struggles, her goodness, her faith. Tell any anecdotes that have been passed down through the ages. If you cannot find a picture of these ancestors, simply use a drawing of a woman of that period. Your daughter will form strong connections with her heritage through this collection.

This can be a great creative writing, history, and religion project for junior and senior high school students. It can be given to a mother from her son or daughter.

Coupons for Mom (S)

Ask children to design coupons and write on them the tasks or household chores they can perform: "Good for cleaning the kitchen for an entire week," "Good for ironing ten articles of clothing," "Good for one back rub," "Good for a week of packed gourmet lunches," and "Good for watering the plants for one month." Redeemable whenever she wishes, these coupons will mean more to Mom than any purchased gift.

Memorial Day

Memorial Day began as a day to honor the nation's war dead. Now this holiday, celebrated on the fourth Monday of May, has expanded to include all those who rest in our cemeteries. Make a visit to an old cemetery today. Enjoy the beauty of the plants and trees. Take some paper and crayons or charcoal pencils and do a collage of gravestone rubbings. Put an American flag on a forgotten soldier's grave and stand in silent prayer for this hero. Read Thornton Wilder's play *Our Town* and meditate on the precious gift of life that we celebrate on this day of memories and honor.

Memorial Stones (F, S)

Create a small centerpiece at home or in the classroom. Collect an assortment of small stones and arrange them in a shallow tray. Put a small American flag in the center. Ask students or family members to write on the stones the names of people they know who have given their lives in service to their country. Encourage viewers of your centerpiece to pick up the stones and pray for the person whose name they hold in their hands.

Visit With a Veteran (S)

In class before Memorial Day have students invite relatives who served in America's wars to visit your class. Ask them to share their experiences and bring any medals, uniforms, mementos, or pictures they may have. This visit brings history right into our midst and is a lasting lesson.

Peacemaking on Memorial Day (F, S)

Spend the day fasting for world peace. Write a letter to your congressional representatives encouraging peace. Plan a prayer experience or liturgy for peace.

Ascension

Whether we look skyward on a Thursday or a Sunday, the message is the same: Jesus wants us to evangelize. On this feast we need to think about getting serious about sharing our faith. It is the moment to reach out to at least three people we know who no longer go to church or have never known Jesus Christ in their lives. Take time today to do something for those three people that could bring them to faith in Christ.

Pentecost

Celebrated as the "birthday" of the church, Pentecost is one of the high points of the liturgical year. But Pentecost has a much older history. It is first a Jewish festival celebrated fifty days after Passover (Deuteronomy 20:1–11). Luke connects the events in the Upper Room with all that has come before. The coming of the Holy Spirit is the climax of Jesus Christ's mission. The Spirit remains with us, as the great gift to the Christian community. Fire and wind are the Spirit's symbols of new life to a weary world. These two symbols vibrate with the pulse of God's presence.

This is a great Sabbath feast. Proclaim a day of rest and play in honor of the Most Holy Playful Spirit. This is Easter's finale. Here are some ways to ring out the last Easter Alleluia.

Play in the Wind (F)

This is another great day to fly a kite (especially if the ocean or lakeshore is near). In keeping with "the spirit" of the day, fly a bird-shaped kite. You may want to build your own and attach a bright pentecostal-red tail. Fly paper airplanes, blow bubbles in the wind, ride in a convertible, hang a wind chime or a wind catcher. Do something to encounter the wind on Pentecost.

Listen to the Wind (F)

Play a flute or pennywhistle or wind instrument. If playing a wind instrument is out of your reach, listen to some flute music. The Native

American musical tradition is rich with wind music. Borrow a recording from the library and commune with the "Great Spirit" who rides the wind. Enter the music of the spirit in the Gaelic tradition as you listen to Irish flute or bagpipes.

Visit the Wind (F)
Go to your favorite windy place. Make a pilgrimage to the lakeshore, mountaintop, farm plains, desert, beach, or even the top of a city building, wherever the sound of wind reigns. Read Acts 2:1–11; sing or recite a few verses of "Come, Holy Ghost" or another hymn to the Holy Spirit. Be as still as you can and simply listen to the wind. Ask the Spirit to fall afresh on you!

Light a Pentecostal Fire (F)
Begin this day as we begin on Holy Saturday. Prepare a bonfire, light a roaring blaze in your fireplace, or simply light a host of candles. Watch the flames dance and entertain you. See the fire anew with a child's eyes. Let the wonder of orange, yellow, and red light warm your spirit. Think about what the fire of the Holy Spirit means to you. Pray for someone who is preparing for or recently celebrated confirmation or pray for the neophytes in your parish.

Wear Red (F)
The color red represents the tongues of fire that rested on the heads of Jesus' followers on the day of Pentecost (Acts 2:1–4). In remembrance of the gift of the Holy Spirit wear red on this feast. Invite everyone in your church to put on red as they worship. The "red" congregation will warm everyone's heart.

Prepare a Pentecost Meal (F)
On this day when the church began, prepare a special Sabbath meal. Invite your confirmation sponsor and godparents. Serve your favorite chili and call it "Flamin' Hot Pentecost Chili." Add to the menu anything that proclaims the day: corn chips and "Spirit" salsa, "fruits of

the Spirit" corn muffins. End the meal with flaming cherries jubilee or a birthday cake loaded with candles!

Saints and Heroes

May 3 • Saint Philip (F, S)

In the gospel stories about Saint Philip, he tries Jesus' patience because he never gets the meaning of what the teacher is saying. Saint Philip was a slow study. He had the passion, the love for Jesus, but he was the last one to understand a parable, struggled with simile, and would be the last one to laugh at a good joke. Do you know one of these lovable souls? In honor of Saint Philip, pray for your own "slow study" today. And, if the spirit inspires you, take him out to lunch, give a bouquet, send an e-mail to let him know that diversity is the spice of life and he is dear to you.

May 10 • Saint Damien of Molokai (F, S)

Saint Damien is new to the ranks of the saints. He was a missionary to the lepers of Hawaii who gave his life to their needs. The native Hawaiians loved this gentle man who taught them more about Jesus Christ by his actions than by his words. On his feast day, create traditional Hawaiian leis in his honor. Make small paper flowers or use silk flowers and string them together as a necklace. Share the story of Saint Damien after you make these Hawaiian symbols of welcome and love.

May 15 • Saint Isidore (F, S)

Saint Isidore is the special keeper of farms and farmers. As you plant your spring garden ask him to help you prosper. It is a custom in many places to create a Mary garden during the month of May. Dedicate your flower or produce garden to "the Mystical Rose." You can place her statue in the midst of the garden and surround her with little stones bearing the names of those whom you would ask her to protect. Ask Saint Isidore to protect and keep this holy space.

Prayers

Hymn to Saint Elizabeth (for the Feast of the Visitation, May 31)

Old beyond hope
you bore the prophet.
Young beyond understanding
your eyes saw only possibilities.
O Elizabeth,
it was your eyes
that made it all come to pass.
Eyes that could see deep within.
Eyes that saw the movement of grace.
Eyes that refused to observe
the world with earthly reason,
cynicism.
Eyes that recognized the unborn Messiah.
O Elizabeth,
teach us how to see.
Let us learn the holy way
you embraced with ease.
Ask God to give us
the grace of clear vision
to see possibilities
instead of dead-ends,
to see hope
in the ashes of failure.
To see Messiah
in a godless world. Amen.

Connection: Reflect on a time in your life when you were over-whelmed with pain, failure, or discouragement. Remember what God did for you in that time. Now, name an area of your present life that you need to see in a new way…God's way. Put a pair of glasses in a visible place to remind you to see your situation with eyes of hope.

Psalm to Welcome a Spring Day
Divine Creator,
your palette of hope
delights the world.
Bare branches are transformed
into pastel laurels of promise.
Pushy, little bulbs
poke out their triumphant blossoms
in pink, yellow, and red.
Renew our winter weary souls
with your flare.
O Timeless One,
create in us the same excitement
we once knew as children.
Jumping with joy over
the pink glory of a blooming flower
the splash of a cherry tree in bloom,
the sweet smell of lilacs.
O Gracious Giver,
of priceless spring,
help us put down our work
and dance with you
as this symphony begins.
For eyes have not seen
the wonder you have ready
for those who take your hand
and step into this marvelous day!

Connection: Open all the windows in your home or classroom this day. Sit in the quiet and feel the gentle breeze. Listen for the sounds of spring: birds chirping, lawn mowers, and children playing.

Prayer After Planting a Garden
Zinnia and Marigold Maker,
we love the work of your hands.
As we lay these seeds and plants
into their bed of promise
grant us the spirit of hope.
This little garden is a sign of your promise
we plant in trust.
You bring forth fruit,
because we believe in the planting.
May the flowers and fruit of this garden
give us sweet delight in the days of summer.
As buds unfold give us the hearts of children
who can see the wonder in it all.
Let us touch,
smell,
see,
your presence in the unfolding grace of a summer garden. Amen.

Psalm at the Waning of Eastertide
Where are you, Risen Lord?
We have seen you in a hundred circling camps,
You have greeted us with the ancient alleluias.
Our hearts were burning with love
when we recognized you in breaking of the bread.
Yet, now, all is quiet.
No longer does the sanctuary
enchant us with its dazzling white.
We have become accustomed to the
grace of resurrection.
The unbelievable is commonplace.
Surprise us this day with your presence
awaken in us a renewed wonder.

Shake the stale alleluia out of our souls
give us the grace of the exalted once again.
May we have eyes to see your movement,
in the commonplace and live Easter always.
Amen.

Connection: Listen to the Hallelujah chorus from Handel's
Messiah. Sing along.

Prayer at Sunset on the Feast of the Ascension
Quietly,
calmly,
with no remarkable effort,
you faded into the sky.
Just as sweetly as the sun now sinks into silence
you left us
ascending into our future.
promising to be with us always.
Even as the sun disappears
we believe it is still warming the earth and keeping us.
You are gone from our vision
yet, evermore
near to us.
Oh Jesus,
may my heart always burn within,
loving you,
without the sight of you.
Serving you,
without seeing your hands.
Speaking of you,
without ever having heard your voice.

I meet with eagerness your
challenge to
"Go make disciples."
I have no skills
only the desire to follow you.
May the setting sun of this holy night
be a reminder that
fire
consumes itself
in the giving of light and warmth. Amen.

Connection: Say this little prayer in the last moments of day-light on the Feast of the Ascension. Choose on this night to carry with you some small reminder that Christ is always with us. Perhaps a small cross in your pocket or around your neck might be the perfect symbol of your communion with the eternal Christ.

Marian Prayer Service
Preparation: Place a vase filled with water in front of a statue of Mary.
Leader: O God, come to our assistance! O Mary, join us!
All: May all the saints and angels be with us as we gather.

Opening Prayer

Blessed Mother, be our advocate this night.
We come to you as children
weary from the world's demands.
Let us rest a while in your maternal arms.
Guide us into union with your son, Jesus.
Scripture: Luke 2:15–19

Reflection and Ritual

Leader: She pondered all these things in her heart. She treasured each little memory. The years brought a return to the ordinary and finally they brought this child of hers to a horrible death. Yet, in all these times she kept, like a shining jewel the visions of her memories.

Have seven participants read the following memories. After each statement, place one of the flowers in the vase in front of the statue. Pause for quiet reflection after each memory.

Angel wings bursting into Morning Prayer with the first "Ave"…

The sweet birth cry in the darkest night of salvation…

Standing with Anna in the temple holding her son and hearing the old woman's words of courage…

Pushing Jesus into action at Cana and reveling in the miracle…

John holding her as she cried on Calvary…

Mary of Magdala rushing toward her saying, "He is alive, he has risen"…

The loud rush of wind blowing open the windows, the exhilaration of the Spirit filling her soul in the Upper Room.

Hymn: Sing together a Marian hymn or listen to an Ave Maria.

Closing Prayer

Mother Mary, little did you know
what God had in store for you.
Yet, your confidence and faith in God never failed.
Lead us into such faith.
Guide us to see the moments of faith in our lives
to ponder and treasure themn as you did.
May your example of simple day-to-day faith
help us to unfold the presence of your son, Jesus
in all we do. Amen.

Connection: Create a May altar in your home. Give Mary a place of honor throughout the whole month, and keep fresh flowers there. Say a Hail Mary each day of May at this spot.

Parish Prayer for First Communion Day
Gathered in your name,
we sense the electric
grace of this day.
Faith is never more potent,
more remarkable,
more wonderful,
than when it shines in the eyes of a child.
As the bread becomes your very essence
we witness the first touch of these children.
The touch,
the reaching out
that marks them forever as one in you.
This sweet communion
is ever more pungent
because we too remember
the first touch.
In innocence and trust
they hold out their hands to you.
We watch as you grab hold of them
with tender love.
Hand in hand the walk begins.
innocence to sophistication,
wonder to commonplace,
in the passing of years
let these little ones
still come to you
with the hearts of children.
May this moment in time
provide enough grace for their eternity. Amen.

Connection: Send a greeting card or note to a favorite child who is making their First Communion. Share the memory of your first Eucharist with this child. You may even like to invite them to share a Sunday Mass and brunch with you in honor of their new privilege.

Mother's Day Litany of Gratitude

Leader: Most High and Holy God, you alone are creator. Yet, you share with all women the making of life. We are grateful for this blessed union. And so we pray:

Leader: For the decision of all mothers to bear our life…

All: We thank you.

Leader: For the nurturing and protections our mothers gave to keep us well…

All: We thank you.

Leader: For the sacrifice of personal pleasure and dreams for the love of their child…

All: We thank you.

Leader: For silently sharing the pain of their child's pain and carrying their burdens with generous hearts…

All: We thank you.

Leader: For their sleepless nights and worry, their prayers and tears…

All: We thank you.

Leader: For the great joy and pride our mothers have in our success.

All: We thank you…

Leader: On this day of reflection and praise for every mother, we ask you to pour out your love and care on our mothers. It is these women who first taught us of your presence, held us as you would hold us, cared for us in your stead. May their holy vocation bring them eternal reward and a shining light in eternity. May their days be marked with untold joy and peace for all they have done. Amen.

Connection: Write a letter to your mother. Tell her your favorite childhood memory of her. Tell her all she means to you. Give it to her with one flower and an embrace.

Prayer for War Memories on Memorial Day
All-powerful God,
who created the world for peace,
remember with us
those who died defending peace.
All that you give us to enjoy,
freedom,
prosperity,
safety,
come to us through the sacrifice
of these dead.
Today, we remember and celebrate
their devotion to the future.
Their vision of a day when peace would dawn
With the every day's rising sun.
Let us never forget
Or take for granted what these
Men and women died for.
In union with you they
Were the bearers of your heart's desire.
Bless them with eternal peace. Amen.

Connection: Celebrate Memorial Day by visiting a war memorial. Say the names of the dead out loud as a prayer. Say it slowly, thinking and praying for the repose of their souls and the well being of their families.

JUNE

Weddings, graduations, festivals, and parties galore fill our calendar as June begins. In the midst of all the uproar the good earth is warming to the first movement of a summer symphony. The overture of May has become a strong melody, and we take the time to see gardens bursting forth and feel the sun warm our face. June is the time to let go of our serious work and dare to rest in the sounds and smells of God's playground. Bare feet splash in streams, picnics bring Eucharist meaning, the sky shines bright, and the smell of freshly mowed grass comes like perfume to our willing senses.

Remembering the Day the Slaves Arrived (June 1) (F)

On June 1, 1619, the first African slaves arrived in Virginia. It marked the beginning of a discrimination that has plagued America for hundreds of years. Today when you pray at meals or in the evening remember those who are children of slavery and discrimination. Ask God to bless and free our country and world from racial injustice.

Father's Day

Father's Day is a perfect opportunity to offer a formal expression of love and appreciation to those who are our fathers. It is not necessary to spend money on a gift and card, yet it is most necessary to remember our fathers with symbols and words. Try these money-free alternatives to express your honor.

Interviews About Fathers (F)

Using a recorder, video camera, or handwritten card ask a young child questions about Dad's life, such as: "Where does your daddy work?" "How old is your daddy?" "What is your daddy's favorite thing to do?"

The answers will delight the unsuspecting dad and be a treasured gift for years to come.

The Begotten Game (F)

A favorite method of discussing lineage in the Old Testament is to describe heritage in terms of who begot whom. So, too, for us it is a great method of discovering our roots by doing the same. Ask each family member to start with his or her own name, followed by the name of the father, for example, "Anne, begotten by William, who...." Each person should then tell one interesting fact about his or her father, such as, "has magnificent brown eyes" or "graduated *magna cum laude* from the University of Michigan." Then, the next person does the same about this man who is the father of this family. In the next round, begin with the father and tell about the grandfather. For example, "William, begotten of Stanley, who fought in France during the Second World War." The next round takes it back another generation. Go back as far as you can with the help of older family members.

Graduation and the End of the School Year

End-of-School Good-bye Box (S)

With the close of each school year comes a bag of mixed emotions. We are glad to be done with the work of school, yet sad to leave good friends. Bring all these emotions into focus by celebrating the end of the year. Ask each student to put into a box one small object that they will not need till next school year (a pen, a lunch money coin purse, a pencil bag). Each article should have the owner's name on it. Seal the box and write on the top, "Things we will need for the first grade" (second, third, fourth, and so on). Give the box to next year's teacher for safekeeping. When school begins the next year, the new teacher can meet her students for the first time by opening the box and calling out the name on each article. (For schools with more than one class per grade, these articles may have to be juggled before the beginning of school.)

Good-bye Seeds (S)

Give each student a packet of seeds to grow during the summer. A good choice is sunflower seeds. They grow easily and provide a natural source of food for local birds. Remind students that as their sunflowers grow toward the sun, so should we use the summer as a time of growth and rest.

Major passages in the lives of family members deserve much notice. It is particularly important for young people to be honored when they complete a step in their education. Graduation is a moment to bask in accomplishments and honors. Here are a few ways to do this.

Create-a-Story Graduation Table (F)

Fill a large table with pictures, trophies, mementos of the school years. You may want to include the school colors, yearbook, and programs. Provide an autograph book and encourage well-wishers to write a comment or congratulatory message.

Teacher Tales (F)

At least six weeks before graduation, send a short note to some of the graduate's favorite teachers. Ask them to write down memories of this student, a message of encouragement and finally, a commendation to go forward using his or her talents. Include a self-addressed, stamped envelope. You may also wish to include letters from coaches, godparents, mentors, pastors, and other significant people. Put all the letters in an album along with the graduation program and any special certificates of honor the graduate has earned. This album will be a treasured memento of this well-earned graduation.

The Graduation Gift (F)

Milestone events present perfect opportunities to give a symbolic gift. The gift becomes a sign of the occasion and a reminder of the grace of the moment. At graduation a perfect gift is a gem. Small semiprecious stones in jewelry, polished rocks, sparkling crystals, make wonderful gifts. These are available at nature stores and other small specialty shops. Accompany this gift with a note that says: "You are a unique gem, a many-splendored wonder. Never has there been, or will there be another like you. Your talents, your intelligence, your laughter, your tears are unique. May this gem always remind you of this day and your accomplishments."

Summer Solstice (June 21) (F)

This is the great sun feast and the longest day of the year. It was an ancient day of song, dance, and feasting. Rise early and wait for the dawn. Stay outside till the last butter-pink rays fade into night. Celebrate the sun today.

Take a Sunbath (F)

Enjoy a break on a park bench, spread a blanket in the park, go to a city rooftop or wherever the sun shines. Slather on the sunscreen and enjoy the warmth of Brother Sun. Read the beautiful "Canticle of the Creatures" composed by Saint Francis of Assisi. Let sunshine invade your soul.

Saints and Heroes

Sacred Heart of Jesus (Third Friday After Pentecost) (F)

This is a feast for true lovers. We remember the heart of Christ in a special way. His Sacred Heart has been the focus of years of Catholic devotion and the special theme of Fridays. The heart of Christ bled to stillness on the cross for the sake of love!

Romans 5:5–11 tells us that this magnificent love is in our hearts, too. In honor of the Sacred Heart of Jesus reach out today to the unloved and suffering. Volunteer to clean up a local soup kitchen. At a hospital chapel, pray for those in the building who are suffering and dying that day. Give money to a homeless person. Do whatever you think the heart of Christ calls you to do. If the Sacred Heart is to keep beating in our world, we must be the workers of love.

On the evening of this feast watch the sky fill with the red of sunset. Let the sky be your hymn of love to the Sacred Heart. See this quick, silent flash of red light as a reminder that love goes on day in and day out through those who have the courage to let one's heart beat with the heart of Christ.

June 12 • Saint Anthony's Vigil (F)

In Portugal on the eve of the feast of Saint Anthony an annual festival is held to celebrate the patron of young lovers. It is a night to honor young love. Tonight, tell the story of your own young love or perhaps the love story of your parents or grandparents.

June 24 • Birth of John the Baptist (F)

We celebrate John's birth on the day when medieval peoples believed that daylight began to decrease. John said, "He [Christ] must increase, but I must decrease" (see John 3:30). This summer birthday invites us to be the lamp of the divine light in the spirit of Saint John.

This is a day of fire and water. The desert man, John, knew these signs so well. Fire and water are the lifeblood of a wanderer. Fire warms and gives light in the desert night; water is the source of new life and refreshment in the desert heat. Build a great fire today and splash in your own "Jordan River."

Plan a family picnic near a riverbank, lakeshore, or seaside. After your meal, build a great fire. See this light as a sacred symbol of God's wonderful love. Take off your shoes and wade in the water. Imagine for a moment that John the Baptizer is with you. Ask this rebel from the desert to help you walk in the footsteps of Christ.

In honor of John, make a desert scene with your children. If you have never visited a real desert, this simple project will get you in touch with the world of the Baptizer. Take a shallow dish and fill it with sand and just a little dirt. Plant a few small cacti in your desert pot. Add a rock or two and maybe even a bone. Put the desert garden in a warm spot and water once a month. Let the little ones touch the prickly cactus skin, sift through the sand, and rub the rocks and dried old bones.

Prayers

Prayer for Fathers, Grandfathers, and Godfathers

O God, whom we call Father, teach us to walk in your image. You who give us life in abundance first breathed life into our lungs as our earthly fathers watched in wonder. Bless these men who care for us: fathers, sires, mentors, men who are made like you. Give them wisdom and courage. In their darkest hours may they know your presence. And may we, those they care for, honor, respect, and revere them, keeping their faces in our prayers and hearts for all eternity. Amen.

Prayer to Fire-Maker God

O Fire-Maker, draw us near to you as we are drawn into these flames. Thank you for this gracious fire that invites us to your love, a blazing reminder of things unseen but always known deep within our spirits. Make this fire a vibrant, worthy blaze. Bless its flames of joy that dance in your love song. The smoke, too, rises high in praise to you. O Holy One, we fill our nostrils with the incense of this fire. Fill us with your Spirit of sweet love, now and forever. Amen.

JULY

Yellow, orange, and red flowers bloom in abundance. The first home-grown tomatoes come to the table. The sun reigns in the blue heaven and life takes on a leisure that encourages time without any thoughts. It is summer in the Western Hemisphere. The season calls us out of our purposeful world and into a place apart with the Spirit of God. Ordinary time invites us to sit and listen to the story of Jesus as he walks the countryside. It is necessary for us to imagine we are with him. That comes easy in the summer sun. Beaches are full of tourists, gardens are full of working hands, and country fairs and festivals are full of excited children. July is meant for the child in all of us to find the Christ in the most ordinary places.

Independence Day

Independence Day is a traditional American day of family, picnics, parades, and fireworks. It is the occasion to celebrate all that is good about freedom and rejoice in this bountiful land. Red, white, and blue bedeck every storefront, commons, and city hall. This secular feast is the occasion of giving thanks to the God "in whom we trust." Pray this prayer as part of your day's festivities.

Organize a Parade (F)

Everyone, especially children, loves a parade. Gather the children of your neighborhood or church with their bikes, wagons, skates, and strollers. Supply plenty of crepe paper, ribbons, and balloons. Decorate all the vehicles. Be sure to include a wagon with an MP3 or CD player loaded with band music and lots of Sousa marches. Put an adult at the beginning and end of the line and here and there in between. March around the block, down the street, or through the town commons. When the parade returns, provide plenty of hot dogs and lemonade to refresh the weary marchers.

"What a State" Picnic (F)

This picnic will help you brush up your geography skills. Invite friends and family to a picnic that features one of the great United States. Display the flag, map, and seal of the chosen state. Serve the native foods of that state (for example, Cajun food for Louisiana, Mexican food for Texas, Dutch food for Pennsylvania). Ask everyone to bring one question about this state. Find out the major industry, largest natural resource, and other statistics and interesting facts. Whoever answers the most questions correctly takes the state flag home. Each July 4 feature a new state. People will reminisce in future years about the 1990 "Utah" picnic or the 1995 "Hawaii" picnic.

Melting Potluck Supper (F)

America is the place where people from every country come to be free. Discover your neighbors' ancestry by having a neighborhood potluck supper in which each family brings a dish from their ancestral land. This patchwork quilt cuisine will give everyone a taste of what "melting pot" really means.

Other Summer Feasts

Rogation Days (F)

In the agricultural world of years past, the church celebrated "rogation" days before Ascension Thursday. The whole community marched in procession through pasture and field singing the litany of the saints, asking the angels and the saints to pray for blessings on the crops.

Remember these ancient prayers and do a little planting. Plant a small garden, a strawberry barrel, a tomato plant, or even a few petunias in a windowbox. The mystery of faith is much like sowing and growing. Plant your seeds and read Mark 4:26–34.

Bastille Day (July 14) (F)

Celebrate the French today. Make French toast. Sip a French wine. Wear a beret. Eat brie. Bake a soufflé. Go to a French restaurant. Learn a French phrase such as, *"C'est la vie,"* or learn to count to twenty in French. Learn to French braid. Rent a French movie. Sing the French national anthem or a French folk song.

First Moon Landing (July 20) (F)

On this date in 1969 Neil Armstrong and Edwin "Buzz" Aldrin, Jr., walked on the moon's surface. In their honor, take your own moonwalk. After nightfall, drive and then walk to a place far from city lights. Find a cozy spot to lay a blanket. Lie back and watch Sister Moon and her friends. Look for the brightest stars. Then try your luck at finding the Big Dipper, the Little Dipper, and Sagittarius. When you return home, listen to *Clair de Lune* by Claude Debussy.

National Ice Cream Day (Third Sunday in July)

President Ronald Reagan proclaimed the ice cream feast in 1984. The president wanted all Americans to celebrate this day by eating the frozen treat with gusto. So on this Sunday, go for a ride in the country and stop at your favorite ice cream spot.

Birthday of Henry Ford (July 30) (F)

Henry Ford was one of the first automobile makers. Plan an adventure in his honor today. Pack a picnic lunch and get into your family car, the great-grandchild of Henry's Model T. Take a day trip to a wonderful little town, state park, historic site, or anywhere your heart desires. There's only one rule: Do it Henry Ford style. Use only back roads—no superhighways!

Saints and Heroes

July 1 • Blessed Junípero Serra

Junípero Serra was a force in the development of present-day California. His missions helped foster the growth of Catholicism in California, and also were important the growth of cities such as San Francisco, San Jose, and San Diego. Serra was instrumental in bringing Christianity to the Native Americans of the Southwest.

July 3 • Saint Thomas the Apostle

Today we honor the famous doubter. It was Thomas who could not believe that Jesus had been resurrected. To be in solidarity with Saint Thomas, make an "I Doubt" list today. Put a piece of paper and a pen on the kitchen table. Ask anyone who sees it to write a sentence that begins with "I doubt...". Talk about the responses together at a family meal. Saint Thomas understands.

July 14 • Blessed Kateri Tekakwitha

Native American Catholics each year hold the National Tekakwitha Conference to build bridges between the Catholic tradition and native heritage. In honor of this saint of the Algonquin tribe, find out more about the Tekakwitha Conference online at www.tekconf.org.

Make a Kateri Bracelet (F)

To remember Blessed Kateri Tekakwitha (and entertain the children of summer), make a unique bracelet. String beads or buttons on cord. Use these colors to symbolize the virtues that Kateri practiced: red for the pain of her suffering for Jesus, green for the hope of eternity with God, black for the courage to outstare the darkness, white for the resurrection of Jesus.

July 16 • Our Lady of Mount Carmel

This feast is a celebration in honor of Our Lady whose first shrine was built at Mount Carmel. She is also known as the Virgin of All Remedies. People come to her shrine to ask for healing and leave replicas of the parts of their bodies which are afflicted. In other parts of the world, her holiday is celebrated with fireworks, parades, and olive branches.

Perhaps this would be a good day to visit the sick, pray for healing, or address an afflicted part of your body.

In the Voodoo tradition, the image of Our Lady of Mount Carmel is used to represent Erzulie Danto, a single mother who is independent, hard-working, and has a fierce temper. "When you see Danto pass by, you say it is a thunderstorm."

July 22 • Mary Magdalene

Mary Magdalene was always there. She stayed with Jesus through his death and was the honored one who first encountered the Risen Christ. Her steadfast love is the hallmark of Christian courage. An ancient story tells that on the first Easter Sunday Mary Magdalene ran to Pilate's house announcing the Resurrection news. Pilate was about to eat a hard-boiled egg as Mary spoke. His retort was that he would believe Jesus had risen from the dead when the egg in his hand turned blood red. In an instant the egg turned red. Pilate at that moment became a believer. Magdalene is often pictured holding a red egg, the first Easter egg. In her honor make "Magdalene Eggs:" Place six hard-boiled, peeled eggs in a jar of pickled beet juice. Let marinate at least four hours and serve.

July 26 • Saints Ann and Joachim

Ann and Joachim are the parents of Mary and the grandparents of Jesus. While we know very little about them, we do know it takes an extended family to form a child—even Jesus. Grandparents have a wonderful role passing on the traditions, faith, and love within the family circle. Ann and Joachim gave Jesus the roots that made his ministry full of love.

Take a moment on their feast to honor your own grandparents or a friend who lives the vocation of grand-parenting with passion. Give them a treat, write them a letter, or send them an e-mail tribute. They are unnoticed heroes, just like Saint Ann and Joachim.

July 29 • Saint Martha

Martha is the patron of cooks. Celebrate hospitality today. Martha was a "doer" and her sister Mary a "be-er." There is a place for both in the faith community. Martha was a Christian activist in the greatest sense. She would teach us to embrace work as prayer.

In the spirit of Saint Martha arrange a "Martha Exchange" for this day. Find another family willing to share their clutter with you. Designate an area that needs cleaning in each of your houses. Then trade chores! For example, your family goes to your friend's house and cleans their garage while they clean your attic. Perform this task as prayer for the family you serve.

Prayers

Freedom Prayer

Great Spirit of Freedom, Firecracker God,
we play before you today.
This is the feast of grateful memories,
of every woman and man who lived to make us free.
May we never forget our wondrous freedom.
Enkindle in us the red fire of your love
so that no one will ever be denied freedom.
Bless this country in the white hope of honor.
May all we do be cloaked in integrity and honesty.
Pour out upon us the blue grace of humility
that we may serve our world with the bounty of America.
We ask this in the name of Jesus Christ
who lives and reigns in perfect freedom forever. Amen.

Rogation Day Prayer

Maker of fruits and flowers,
bless this work we do.
Creator of fruits and flowers,
kiss the earth and bless our seeds.
May the promise of fertile crops tended by our hands
remind us of your power to bring forth fruit
and your promise to keep those you love in abundance.
Amen.

Prayer for Summer Silence
Into the place of deep quiet,
my soul flees.
The clamor of my noisy life
drowns out
the voice of God.
Deep blue,
shimmering
waters of silence,
I dive
dive,
dive,
into this pool
of *Sancte Spiritu.*
Oh, little swimmer,
resist the urge
to speak.
Allow the sweet,
wet,
silence,
to cover you.
Wordless depths
of healing.

Connection: Find some time to go to a quiet place by the water. Sit in the stillness; resist the urge to speak to God. Simply be very still and know that God is with you.

AUGUST

As the dog days of summer fill the August landscape our spiritual landscape slows into the warm haze of soft conversations in the parables of ordinary time. It is a time of stillness, a time of ease. Brother Sun reigns in his throne and Sister Moon dances in the night sky. Creation is boasting about God's power.

Our hearts begin to stir with a call to readiness. Vacations end, school notices arrive, the first hint of harvest reminds us that summer cannot last forever. The lazy days of peaceful leisure are waning. We hesitate to leave our lawn chairs and tall, cool drinks for the tools of harvest. Hesitation is a grace in itself.

Columbus Sails for the New World (August 3) (F)

Do you have a hard time facing the unknown? In honor of Columbus's courage, why not get lost today? Take the family on a drive on the expressway. Get off at an unknown exit and try to get home using smaller roads and no map. If you are not quite up to high adventure, honor this ancient navigator by making a balloon-powered boat.

Cut away one side of a cardboard milk carton. Cut the end off a bendable straw so the bend is centered between the two ends. Tape one end of the straw inside a balloon. Poke a hole big enough for the straw in the bottom of the carton. Put the balloon inside the carton with the straw protruding through the hole. Bend the straw upwards at a right angle (the propeller) outside the carton. Blow up the balloon and hold the end of the straw. Place in water and let go of the straw. Off she blows!

Hiroshima Day (August 6) (F)

What a horror this day was for the people of Japan. Thousands died, thousands suffered in the end of a hateful war. In the name of those who died, put a single flower on your supper table. Stand around the table before the meal and observe a minute of silent prayer for the victims of the first atomic bomb.

Visit a Farmer's Market (F)

In Europe this is a harvest festival. Have your own festival. Find a local produce stand, farmers' market, or even the produce section of your local grocery. Select a wide variety of fresh fruits and vegetables, then go home and prepare your harvest. Serve up tomatoes, corn, beans, cucumbers, melons, and berries. Leave an empty chair at the table and invite the Blessed Mother to join you.

Tomato Days

There is nothing like the taste of homegrown tomatoes. Everyone is happy to receive the surplus from friends who planted too many plants in the enthusiasm of spring planting. One of my favorite ways to eat them comes from Mrs. Murphy, my childhood neighbor. She called it "poor woman's hors d'oeuvres." Spread a little peanut butter on a butter cracker, and top it with a chunk of tomato and a little salt. Pop it in your mouth. Mmm.

Saints and Heroes
August 6 • The Transfiguration (F)

The summer sun is at its most glorious in the northern hemisphere at this time of year. There is no more fitting time to tell the story of Elijah, Moses, and Jesus transformed in radiant glory. We are invited to go to the mountaintop to see God, the law, and the prophets. Spend some time in a quiet place with Jesus the Christ today. Adore him. Say nothing. Simply bow in profound reverence before him who is "Light from Light, true God from true God." Read Mark 9:2–10. Then leave your quiet place, your own "holy mountain." As you return to the world, keep his divine presence in your heart.

August 10 • Saint Lawrence (F)

Lawrence was a deacon who died a martyr's death in 258, professing his love for Christ while his murderers grilled him. His devotion to God, despite the horrors that faced him, is an example that lives on in countless deacons in today's church. The permanent diaconate is a source of spiritual wealth to us all. If your church has a deacon, or you know one, pick a bouquet of summer flowers and take them to him with a note of thanks.

August 12 • Saint Clare (F)

Saint Clare of Assisi followed Francis' footsteps and embraced poverty and simplicity. She founded the order of the Poor Clares. Clare's spirit is still with us today in the lives of thousands of Franciscan sisters and women of the Franciscan Third Order. In honor of Clare's call to simplicity and poverty, empty your clothes closets today. Give away everything that doesn't fit or that you have not worn in one year. Take your clothing to the nearest St. Vincent de Paul Center or local outlet for the poor. Resolve to live more simply. Ask Clare's advice in those areas of your household and personal life that need trimming.

August 15 • Mary, on the Feast of the Assumption

Today we celebrate Mary's final journey into heaven. This is a most blessed occasion. There is sweetness in the air. Mary becomes for all eternity our mother in heaven. We celebrate her purity, her beauty, and the wonder of the gift she gave us, Jesus. In many countries this is a harvest festival day. In the middle of August most of the Northern Hemisphere is bursting with flowers, vegetables, and fruit.

Make an Altar (F)

Find a picture or statue of Mary and place it in a prominent place in your home—the family room coffee table, the porch table, the kitchen table, wherever people gather. Place a bouquet of flowers and a small candle in front of your Mary. Before supper, gather together, light your candle, and say the Hail Mary.

August 24 • Saint Bartholomew
Saint Bartholomew was an afterthought. He came into the roster of apostles with the exit of Judas. While we know little about him, anyone who made the team at the last moment can claim him as a patron. In Europe many markets and fairs are held on his feast, such as Smithfield, London, where the Bartholomew Fair performs Ben Jonson's comedies. To celebrate this Johnny-come-lately, visit a state fair, a local fair, or a parish festival.

August 27 • Saint Monica (F)
Monica was the mother of Saint Augustine. It is said that her persistent prayers are responsible for the conversion of this great saint. Whom or what do you pray for? Today, spend a little time with your mother, grandmother, or godmother. Thank her for all she does for you. Be sure to talk to Saint Monica, too, about all your unanswered prayers.

August 28 • Saint Elizabeth Seton (F)
Elizabeth Seton, born on this day in 1774, was an American woman whose courage and faith brought the gospel to the young American church. She practiced charity as her special concern and founded the Sisters of Charity. In Elizabeth's honor, perform a few secret acts of love today: Pay the toll for someone behind you at a tollbooth or on the bus, take donuts to your neighborhood fire station, mow your neighbors' lawn. Go out looking for charity today!

Prayers
Phony Baloney Psalm
O Font of Eternal Truth,
why is it so hard to be honest with ourselves?
Why do we embellish and
alter the truth.
May we believe in honesty.
What is so hard about seeing
through your eyes?

Tomato Psalm
Red tomato Maker,
I praise you
for little surprises of warm sweetness
called Big Boy, Little Girl, Heritage Rose—
each a splendid burst of your hand.
You alone could master these treasures of summer.
Let me never take for granted the work of your hands.
from soaring mountains to little tomatoes
your wonders are magnificent!

SEPTEMBER

September is the season of harvest. The fields are full of produce, the fruit trees are laden with sweet apples, peaches, pears, and figs. The vineyards are ripening. The bountiful hand of the divine one is tempting us all with savory and sweet surprises.

This is the perfect moment to teach children the connection between planting seeds and harvesting the gift. Whether it is in the world of earth and seed or the spiritual realm of the fertile ground of tiny souls, the signs of harvest time teach more than any lecture. This month of late summer is full of teaching moments for everyone. Ordinary time gives us the Word with renewed rigor as we get closer to the character of Jesus in these gospels of challenging truth and passionate love. There is wisdom in this September time that gives us grounding in the mystery of the fading blooms and the spent garden.

Celebrate the Harvest

Visit an Apple Farm (F, S)

Take a class trip or a family outing to a local pick-your-own apple farm. (If you live in an area where apples do not grow, go for a ride into the country with a bag of your favorite apples!) This activity encourages everyone to get outside and enjoy the quiet beauty of God's good earth. Pick several different varieties. Encourage children to taste the difference in various types of apples. When you return home with your supply, make apple pie or another favorite apple treat together. When everyone has finished eating, impress them with your wisdom by saying, "Anyone can count the seeds in an apple, but only God knows how many apples are in a seed!"

Apple Tasting (S)

Hold an apple tasting. Let children taste and identify different varieties of apples. You can easily integrate this activity into a science lesson.

Explain that God's people are like the many varieties of apples—we have many differences that make us unique, but we all belong to the same species. Share with the class this simple analogy: The apple's skin is like God the Parent—it protects the apple from disease and harm; the pulp is like Jesus—it is our nourishment; the seeds are like the Spirit—they hold the promise and hope of growth.

Plant Spring Bulbs (F, S)

Fall is a time of seeding. This cycle holds abundant lessons. We reap what we sow, the saying goes. Let yourself and those you nurture get in touch with the simple yet profound meaning of nature's process. We are called to plant spiritual, emotional, and even physical seeds so that we might know life in abundance.

Purchase a variety of spring bulbs. Compare the different sizes and shapes. Dig holes the required depths and let the children hide spring's promise in its winter nest. Bury the bulbs with dirt and mulch them with dried leaves.

If you live in a climate where bulbs won't grow or you have limited space, you can do this indoors by burying the bulbs in a large clay pot and covering them with potting soil. Put the pot in a cold, dark place till Ash Wednesday. Then bring the pot into a warm, sunny location. Water, keeping the soil lightly moist. Watch spring unfold in your house or classroom. As the blossoms appear, let your nose soak up the sweet aroma of spring. Easter will be filled with the sign of new life promised in the autumn planting.

When all the bulbs are safely hidden in their winter sanctuary, share cups of hot cider, herbal tea, or hot chocolate. Reflect on the passage of time and the ways we plant promises of new life by our actions.

The Mustard Seed (S)

Gather a large collection of seeds. Ask everyone to bring something different to your collection. See how many varieties of pods and seeds you can find. Look at the differences, and talk about the wonder of plant reproduction.

Explore the methods by which seeds are pollinated (this might be integrated with a science lesson). Emphasize how God continues to create new life in the marvelous drama of nature's cycle.

Celebrate the seeds of autumn in a paraliturgy. Read the first creation story in Genesis (1—2:4). Then ask children to come forward one by one with their favorite seeds. Let them describe their seeds as they place them before a lighted candle.

After each seed is presented, the leader says, "For this promise of life and hope of creation, we say," and everyone answers, "We thank you, Lord."

Then read together the parable of the mustard seed (Matthew 13:31–32). Remind children of the large plants promised in these seeds and of their own potential as they grow. Close with this prayer:

> God of everything created,
>
> bless and prosper our earth.
>
> Teach us to care for every seed you send.
>
> May these little seeds we hold in our hands
>
> be signs of hope, signs of wonder for us.
>
> May we never forget your care and love for us.

Making Buckeyes

In the Northern Hemisphere there is a stately tree that children love to climb to collect its seeds. The buckeye or horse chestnut tree is an easy climb and its fleshy pods are a delight to open. Within the pod is a beautiful woody seed the size of a walnut. In Britain the buckeye is called a "conker" and is used in a children's game. In honor of this kid-friendly tree a candy was created to imitate the seed of the buckeye tree. Buckeye candy is easy to make and a wonderful treat after a tree-climbing expedition on a September Saturday. Children can have a hands-on cooking experience making these treats:

Candy Buckeyes

1 cup butter

4 cups confectioners' sugar

1/2 tsp. vanilla extract

1-1/2 cups creamy peanut butter

4 cups semisweet chocolate chips

Mix first four ingredients in a saucepan over low heat. Form into walnut-size balls and cool.

Melt chocolate in a double boiler. Dip candy balls in the chocolate mixture, so that the resulting candy resembles a buckeye. Let harden on wax paper. This candy can be frozen.

Labor Day

This national holiday of rest is the official end of summer. It is celebrated on the first Monday in September. Say good-bye to summer with a picnic. Decorate with laborers' hats: hard hats, fire hats, nurses' caps, police hats, and so on. Ask everyone to answer these questions: When you were eight years old, what did you want to be when you grew up? Name all the jobs you have had. If you could work at anything now, what would it be?

In years past, Labor Day marked the end of summer. White shoes, purses and hats were put away, the swimming pools closed and everyone buckled down for work and school. While summer goes by all too fast, September is a great time to celebrate a return to more productive activities.

Farewell-to-Summer Picnic (September 22) (F)

September 22 is the last day of summer. Celebrate the close of the season with a farewell picnic. Serve lemonade, popsicles, and typical summer fare. Get a large box and let everyone fill it with the things you won't be using till next June: suntan lotion, beach toys, flip-flops. Toss water balloons or run through a lawn sprinkler. Say good night to summer by catching the last fireflies or picking the last blooms from the garden or looking at summer vacation photos or whatever says, "It's over" for you. Offer a family prayer of thanksgiving for the summer you have just shared.

Back to School

Autumn brings to a sudden halt the laziness of summer days. As classrooms reopen their doors and families go back into high gear, we look at these last days of summer as a source of consolation and enjoyment. Family, school, and church activities begin anew. As bathing suits and beach towels give way to sweatshirts and soccer balls, we look to autumn as a time to reenter life, to get involved again after the summer sabbatical. Whether you are called to motivate the "child of summer" in your classroom or rejuvenate the family spirit after the dog days of August, these activities will spark everyone's interest.

School Supplies (F)

Set aside a time to go shopping for all those erasers and glue sticks your students need. While some children love to get ready for the first day of school, others dread it. Turn the preparation time into a positive experience for everyone. After the shopping is complete, take some time together over pizza or a sundae to talk about the good things that happen as we return to school. Reassure your children that getting back into the discipline of school life isn't easy, but it is an important part of growing into adulthood. Be there to listen to their fears and offer support as they spend this time with you.

Gifts for the Teacher (F)

Students throughout the world start school at this time. In Russia, students bring their teachers flowers. In Myanmar, the traditional gift on the first day of school is a coconut or banana. Help your children think of simple, creative gifts for their teachers at the beginning of the school year.

Home From the First Day of School (F)

Plan a special after-school snack to greet your tired students as they come home. If you are working and your children come home to an empty house, prepare a little surprise: Write a little love note, promising some special time when everyone comes together at the end of your working day.

Listen to their tales of woe and joy. Be sure to ask the classic questions: "Where is your desk?" "Who is your teacher?" "Did everyone return this year?" "Are there any new people?" "What is your favorite class going to be?" When you finish this time together, give each of your children the kind of hug God gives us to show divine delight in all we do. Remember that you are God's arms for your child.

Pack a Learning Lunch (F)

The same old brown bag with the regular fare gets boring and dull after the first week or two. Try offering a "food of the week" theme. For example, you might use apples to make apples and caramel dip, applesauce, and apple-and-cheese kabobs. You can do something similar with nuts, veggies, potatoes, and so on.

Another way to perk up school lunches is to include an occasional little surprise in the lunchbox, a sprinkling of love. Like the fast food restaurant kids' meals, include a new eraser, a funny joke, a bookmark.

You might decorate a plain brown bag with a colorful sticker and a current events question from the morning paper. The question can be answered at the evening supper table as the opening topic of conversation.

A "Here We Are!" Celebration (S)

A new teacher, new schedules, perhaps even a new school, can make the beginning of school tense and difficult. New shoes, new faces, new clothes change the texture of the day. Ease the adjustment by having a "Here we are!" celebration.

Ask each student to interview another student (preferably someone they do not know well) by asking five "favorite" questions such as:

What is your favorite color?
What is your favorite food?
What is your favorite sport?
What is your favorite animal?
What is your favorite song?

Have each student introduce the person interviewed by telling the class some of those favorites. After this experience spend some time in prayer giving thanks for one another. You may wish to plan a prayer service to conclude this time. Older students could plan this closing rite themselves.

Posters About Us (S)

Ask students to make posters about themselves. Include photographs, vital statistics, and lots of other favorites such as hobbies, talents, great trips. Hang these posters around the classroom. During the first few weeks of school, perhaps during religion class, ask one or two students each day to explain their posters.

These simple exercises build community and ownership in your classroom. As each person tells his or her story, a bond begins to form among students. They become a unique group. The "fifth grade class" is no longer a nondescript group. They become a blend of favorites and gifts like no other before them. Conclude these introductory classes by selecting a class symbol or name like "Ms. Morgan's Marvelous Marauders."

Eid ul-Fitr (September 9) (F, S)

Eid ul-Fitr is a Muslim holiday that marks the close of Ramadan, the Islamic month of fasting. With the appearance of the crescent moon Muslims break their fast and celebrate three days of festivity. Take a moment to learn more about the Muslim faith. Do you know the Five Pillars of Islam? Therein lies a good lesson for all of us.

National Hispanic Heritage Month (F, S)
Our Catholic Church in the Americas has a large percentage of Spanish-speaking members. This month is a great time to learn a little more about the foods of Hispanic culture. Have a Mexican buffet during this month. There are plenty of cookbooks that have wonderful Mexican recipes.

Rosh Hashanah (F, S)
Discover the meaning of the Jewish New Year. Research the customs of this Jewish holiday such as sounding the shofar (ram's horn). A class could invite a local rabbi or Jewish friend to share and demonstrate the Hebrew rituals of this holiday.

Saints and Heroes
September 8 • Mary's Birthday
Mother Mary has a birthday just like the rest of us. What a realization to remember that she is a very human woman who was born and lived an ordinary life until she met up with the angel Gabriel. On her nativity day make a cake with blue candles and sing to her. You can sing "Happy Birthday" or perhaps a favorite Marian hymn.

September 15 • Our Mother of Sorrows
The feast of Our Mother of Sorrows reminds us of Mary's enormous grief. She is seen on this feast as the Mary of the Pieta holding the body of Jesus. Every mother who has lost a child can turn to Mary for help. On this feast day reach out to a mother you know who carries sorrow in her heart for a dead child. Send her a note, take her flowers, and pray for her.

September 23 • Saint Padre Pio
Saint Padre Pio is a new saint with an old story. He said, "Pray…and don't worry." In honor of the holy Capuchin friar, make a worry list today. Write down all the things that keep you awake at night. Put the list in the back of your Bible and imagine you are placing it in God's

hands. In three months, make plans to retrieve the list and give thanks for all the worries that ended because of prayer.

September 27 • Saint Vincent de Paul
"A little charity goes a long way" could be the motto of Saint Vincent de Paul. He worked tirelessly for the poor and his real motto was "God sees you." Can you imagine how charitable we would all be if we remembered that God is watching? In celebration of his feast make a donation to the Saint Vincent de Paul Society.

September 28 • Good King Wenceslas
The good king has been long forgotten since we last sang his tune at Christmastime. To honor him as something besides the Christmas saint, look up his story and celebrate his accomplishments. He is known for making footprints in the snow. In his honor make a Wenceslas Slushy.

> *Wenceslas Slushy*
> Blend together:
> 1 cup sugar
> 1 (6 oz.) frozen orange juice
> 1 (6 oz.) frozen pink lemonade
> 6 cups of water
> 1 can crushed pineapple
> Pour into covered container and place in the freezer. Store and serve when it gets slushy.

September 29 • The Archangels
The feast of Michael, Raphael, and Gabriel is referred to as "Michaelmas" in many countries and is a celebration of the harvest. In England this day was the occasion of "quarter days," on which servants were hired and school terms began. Europeans know this day as the start of the hunting season. In Germany, Austria, and Denmark, Michelsminne, a special wine, is drunk on this day. On Michaelmas the

food is unique: In England they eat goose for prosperity, in France Gaufres, a waffle, in Scotland they are tempted with scones called Struan Micheil, and in Italy the archangels are celebrated with gnocchi. Learn the Prayer to Saint Michael by heart and as a reward have a scone, a waffle, or whatever is sweet to the palate.

Prayers

Good-bye-to-Summer Prayer
Creator God,
as the last summer sun folds into the horizon,
we thank you for being our companion in this season.
Was it you we heard laughing as we splashed in cool waters?
Was it you who made the sweet smell of newly mown grass?
Was it you twinkling a smile in the night stars?
Yes! Oh yes! It was you!
We are grateful, God, that you took time
to journey through summer with us.
As the night bleeds into autumn,
we await the surprise of your next step. Amen.

September Gathering Prayer
Focus: September is the time of harvest and the beginning of the school year. These two themes compliment each other as we consider that each harvest is the fulfillment of hard work and faithfulness. Each harvest has its beginning in the planting of seeds and brings forth life in abundance. When God calls us "the apple of my eye" it tells us that God is willing to tend to our needs, encourage and love us so that we might have fullness of life.
Preparation: Create a prayer space with a large bowl of apples (enough for all present), a lighted candle, and an open Scripture. You may add autumn flowers or any seasonal decoration. Place these symbols on a dark, green cloth representing ordinary time. Have music ready for a quiet reflection time.

Opening Prayer

Apple-Maker God

We praise you for the fruits of September.
Long into the greening of the summer earth
you bring us a sign of your love,
fruit beyond measure
apples tell us that the promise is true!
Apples become the gift of that promise—
signs of love in the making.
We receive your little gifts
in grateful remembrance
of your constant care.

Scripture: Deuteronomy 32:7–12

Reflection and Prayer

Remember the days of old,
consider the years long past;
Ask your father and he will inform you.
Ask your mother and she will tell you stories.
The Lord's own portion was his people;
Jacob his allotted share.

■ ■ ■ ■ ■ ■ ■

OCTOBER

October bursts on the horizon as a shining light. God's splendor is in full array in hues of orange, red, and gold. Nothing can match an autumn landscape. Even in other parts of the hemisphere, October hints at things to come. Life is slowing into sleep. The days are full of bittersweet moments: Trees lose their leaves even as they are splashed with color, grass fades into brown, animals hide in their winter nests. Yet, it is the grace of change that soaks into our souls. It is a fine beginning to a winter's tale and our hearts must be ready to receive it. October is that last burst of deep green ordinary time that reveals a God who remains and even dances with us, if we have the courage to accept the divine tune.

October offers a more somber note. Even as we delight in the joyous color, in the water that comes to the thirsty desert, in the ocean quieting into winter's peace, we realize that the end is near. Soon the earth will lie in a quiet deathlike sleep. In the stark darkness of winter, we find a bittersweet joy. In the changing seasons we know this truth of every life: For every moment of delight and joy, for every birth, we encounter some pain, some sorrow, some death. The balance of this cycle calls us ever deeper into the mystery of our own redemption. Into our pain comes the promise of new and greater life. Even as the earth falls into death, the sweet promise of another spring lies hidden in the dark earth. Jesus invites us into the ageless journey of the paschal mystery. Let us enter into the wonder of the season.

Leaf Saturday (F)

This autumn celebration won't be found on many calendars but is a delightful way to welcome autumn for those who live in climates where the trees change colors. On the Saturday when the leaves are at their autumn brightest take a trip to a nearby park or forest for a visual feast of color. Pick the brightest leaves for your collection as you enjoy a vigorous hike. When you return home, dip your leaves in melted paraffin for a lasting reminder of your day among the trees.

Make leaf cookies for a "Leaf Saturday" dessert. Cut sugar cookie dough in the shape of leaves. When they have baked and cooled, ice them with splotches of red, yellow, orange, brown, and green icing. This hands-on activity allows everyone a share in the Artist's handiwork.

Collecting Leaves (S)

Let the children bring to class the most colorful leaves from home. Discuss the way each leaf is fashioned similarly and yet each leaf has a particular beauty. Point out that God creates a many-splendored variety of both leaves and people. Allow the children to talk about their favorite colors and to describe the colors God gave them: eyes, hair, skin, and so on. Write a litany of thanksgiving naming all the colors God has given this class. Use this litany in a prayer service or liturgy during these fall days.

A simple art project will reinforce the lesson of particular beauty. Dip leaves in poster paint and press on absorbent white paper. Vary color and pattern for better effect. Let children create their own designs using the autumn colors they have seen in the leaves. You might add a Scripture verse or a prayer of thanksgiving for creation to these paintings. These colorful paintings bring the wonder of the season into the room and remind us of the love and artistry of our delightful God.

Halloween

Halloween's roots lie in an ancient pagan festival for the dead. While this autumn feast can be used for evil purposes, our culture celebrates it as an innocent night of begging and fun. We who believe in the light of the world can use it to celebrate the light. *Hallow* means "holy" and the word *Halloween* refers to the night before the feast of all holies, or All Saints' Day. Emphasize all things good, joyful, and pure. Let your children know that they are "children of the light" called to walk in the light.

Costume Box (F)

Get a head start on Halloween preparations by spending an afternoon gathering dress-up goodies for your trick-or-treaters. Put old, funny-looking clothing, wigs, makeup, whatever you find in a box. On the day of Halloween get out your box and let children create their own characters. Encourage them to be funny and outrageous.

Halloween Party (F)

As an alternative to letting your children go begging, try hosting a party for your children and their friends. Give each child an empty bag. Let the partygoers earn their treats by performing nice tricks for the adults. Be sure to provide lots of nutritious snacks for the bags as well as a few sweet surprises. Carve pumpkins, bob for apples, have a bonfire, enjoy the beauty of the autumn night without worrying about your children's safety.

Family Saints (F)

Since this is the night before All Saints' Day, it is a great idea to explore the family saints. Let your children find out who their patron saints are and why they are so honored. They may even choose to dress up like Joan of Arc, George the Dragonslayer, or Francis of Assisi. They could have fun letting their friends guess who they are by giving clues about their saint's life...for a treat of course!

Pumpkin Farm Visit (F)

Take a trip to a pumpkin farm or country market to pick out the family pumpkin. Take along a loaf of pumpkin bread (see recipe below) and a jug of apple cider. When you get home with the family pumpkin(s), ask everyone to draw faces on paper. Let the family vote on the winning face(s) before the carving begins.

Pumpkin Bread Recipe
1 2/3 cup flour
1 1/4 cup sugar
1 teaspoon baking soda
1/2 teaspoon cinnamon
1/2 teaspoon nutmeg
1/4 teaspoon salt
2 eggs
1/2 cup vegetable oil
1/3 cup water (or less)
1/2 cup chopped nuts
1 cup pumpkin

Mix dry ingredients; add nuts. Mix in egg, oil, water, and pumpkin. Stir until blended. Bake in a greased loaf pan (9" x 5" or 10" x 4") 60 to 70 minutes in a preheated 350-degree oven.

Candle Blessing (S)

Whenever an opportunity arises to combine the sacred and the secular to enrich your students' faith, take advantage of it. Halloween provides just such an opportunity. Children have horrible, unspoken fears about things that go bump in the night. This occasion is a perfect time to teach the simple gospel truth that the light does indeed outshine the darkness.

Ask each child to bring a candle to class. Clean out the inside of a large pumpkin. Carve a smiling face on the pumpkin. Talk about the joy of laughing together. Tell students that smiles, laughter, and joy are simple gifts that God gives us to erase sadness and fear. Ask them how they feel when they see a scary pumpkin. How do they feel when they look at this smiling one? Decide together which one is the most like God. Then share with the class the wonder that each of us has within us the power to be a light just like Jesus. We become a light that can erase hatred, evil, pain, and sadness. The light in us is just like Jesus' light. Put a large candle in your smiling jack-o'-lantern. Darken the room if possible. Watch the flame as it fills the pumpkin and lights the room. Notice how much more intense the smile becomes with the light shining through. Ask children to hold their candles in front of them while you say this blessing:

God who created pumpkins and people,
bless our beautiful Halloween light.
This light reminds us that Jesus is the light of the world.
Jesus shines through the darkness
and turns the night into day,
sadness into joy,
hate into love
and tears into smiles.
Bless the candles that we hold.
Let them be a reminder that we are your candles
lighting up the smiles and hearts of our friends and family.
Bless the happy pumpkins we will carve for our candles,
that everyone who sees them might never be afraid of the darkness
because your wonderful Light is with us.

You might close this prayer service with a rendition of "This Little Light of Mine" or another hymn about light.

Saints and Heroes
October 1 • Saint Thérèse of the Child Jesus
The Little Flower, as she thought of herself, teaches us the "Little Way." She was a young French Carmelite nun who never left the confines of her monastery in Lisieux, France, yet she became a doctor of the church and answered millions of prayers. She taught us to do small things each day for love of the Jesus and to be childlike in trust and dependence on God. That is wisdom for today. Saint Thérèse liked to keep five beans in her left pocket. Each time she did some act of love

she transferred a bean to her right pocket. Her goal was to get all the beans in her right pocket each day.

In honor of this amazing nun, put five pennies, beans, or buttons in your left pocket and try to do five acts of love to get those beans on the right side.

October 2 • Feast of the Guardian Angels

All children love knowing that they have their own angels. Their angels are lifetime friends who are there to light and guide their way. There is an old medieval tale that says if you ask your angel its name, the first name that comes to mind is its name. It is great fun to have little ones draw a picture of their guardian angel and then sit quietly, looking at the picture and say, "What's your name, angel?" Then write the name on the drawing. Then say the Guardian Angel Prayer and add their name.

October 4 • Saint Francis of Assisi

Saint Francis was a radical disciple. He walked away from a secure life to an insecure one and never looked back. He was not the birdfeeder statue that we find in our gardens. His gentleness and passionate love for Jesus guided him to live the gospel with a new energy that began a legacy that is called Franciscan spirituality. Spend some time outdoors today. Greet Brother Sun and Sister Moon, Brother Fire and Sister Water. In Saint Francis' honor, think of something you can do to protect and preserve the earth. Call this list your "Canticle list" and keep adding to it.

October 18 • Saint Luke

This day marks the onset of summer-like days that are the last warm weather until spring (just like the Indian summer that is officially dated as November 11 through 20). Luke's "Little Summer" was named to honor the feast of Saint Luke which always seemed to by a warm day of festive outdoor celebrations. Everyone knew that the writer of this Gospel was responsible for the fine warm weather on his feast. Plan an outdoor lunch or supper to honor Saint Luke. Wear your summer sandals for the last time. With nightfall, put away your summer shoes for another year.

October 19 • Saints Isaac Jogues, John de Brébeuf, and Companions

These French Jesuits were brave beyond telling. They were the first missionaries to Canada and North America. Isaac Jogues, John de Brébeuf, Gabriel Lalemant, Noel Chabanel, Charles Garnier, Anthony Daniel, Rene Goupil, and John de Lalande (the first six Jesuits, the last two laymen) came to the Iroquois and Huron Indians, and after being tortured, they were martyred in the area of Auriesville, New York. They died between 1642 and 1649. But their deaths were not in vain. In fact only ten years after their deaths Kateri Tekakwitha was born in the same village in which Saint Isaac Jogues was martyred.

Prayers
Evening Prayer on the Feast of Saint Francis
This evening prayer is designed with children in mind. As the sun is setting, families are invited to gather together around an outdoor statue of Saint Francis.

Preparation: The children are asked to prepare by creating a drawing of their favorite pet, zoo animal, forest creature. These drawings should be on poster board attached to dowels so they can be stuck in the ground around the statue.

Leader: Let us be still and listen to the sounds of creation as the sun begins to set.
Let there be a short period of silence.

Opening Prayer
As the shadows of the evening stretch across the earth, we remember Saint Francis who taught us how to praise God in the simple beauty of all creation. Francis knew that the kingdom of God is in our midst, if we have but the eyes to see and the ears to hear. Listen to his words of praise:

Canticle of the Creatures

Side One: Most high, all powerful, all good, Lord! All praise is yours, all honor and all blessing.

Side Two: To you alone, Most High, do we belong. No mortal lips are worthy to proclaim your name.

Side One: All praise be yours, my Lord, through all you have made, and first my Lord, Brother Sun, who brings the day and the light you give to us through him.

Side Two: How beautiful is he, how radiant in all his splendor! Of You, Most High he bears a likeness.

Side One: All praise be yours, my Lord through Sister Moon and Stars. In the heavens you have made them, bright, precious, and fair.

Side Two: All praise be yours my Lord, through Brother Wind and Air, and fair and stormy all the weather's moods by which you cherish all that you have made.

Side One: All praise be yours, my Lord through Sister Water. So useful, lowly, precious, and pure.

Side Two: All praise be yours, my Lord, for Brother Fire, through whom you brighten up the night. How beautiful he is, full of power and strength!

Side One: All praise be yours, my Lord through Sister Earth our mother, who feeds us in her sovereignty and produces flowers, fruits, and herbs to feed us.

Side Two: Praise and bless my Lord and give him thanks and serve him with great humility.

Hymn: "He's Got the Whole World in his Hands"
Sing two verses using "Sun and Moon" and "Wind and the Rain"...

Litany of Intercession

Leader: God has given us all creation to enjoy and preserve. Let us ask a blessing of all those little creatures who provide companionship and love and ask so little in return:

Each child is now invited to come forward with their poster and proclaim:
"God bless_____(the name of the animal)"
All: "Lord hear our prayer."
The child places the dowel in the ground so that the posters are around the statue.

Closing Prayer

God of all creation, we pause as night falls to give thanks and remember all you have given us. May your servant and our brother Saint Francis be with us tonight as we ask a blessing on our families. Teach us to value the small things, to learn to live with less in the spirit of this good saint. May his love for you be an example to us. May we learn to notice you in all things especially the earth and its beauty. Amen.
Closing Hymn: "He's Got the Whole World in His Hands." *Sing two verses using "Fire and the Water" and "You and me Brother…"*

Connection: Create a winter-feeding center for the urban animals. Perhaps a bird feeder, bird bath, or a container of feed corn for "Brother Squirrel."

Prayer on the Feast of Our Mother of Sorrows
You were warned
Most Holy Virgin,
that your "yes"
would bring pain.
Yet, still we celebrate
all that was given you.
Loneliness into eternal union,
fear into trust,
anxiety into lasting peace,
rejection into profound honor,

pain into wholeness,
humiliation into universal respect,
grief into everlasting life.
Mother Mary,
these seven swords
are indeed two-edged.
Come to our sides
and teach us the
way of your sorrow.
May we believe with you
that the piercing sword
will be transformed
into grace. Amen.

NOVEMBER

The earth is settling into silence. Whether you are near the ocean, the desert, or the mountains, earth is giving us signals of sleep in the Northern Hemisphere. We can take these signs to heart and allow our own bodies to slow into quiet. It is good to sense the wind changing, the birds migrating, green things fading, and animals headed into hibernation. It is the season of reflection on a good harvest, a time to put closure on the work of the fields and fold our hands in gratitude. The church enters the last weeks of the liturgical year. We hear the warnings of the end time and sermons get somber and serious. November brings us a feast of paradise, All Saints' and Souls', and ends with a flourish as we proclaim Jesus king.

All Saints' Day (November 1) (S)

An exercise for the school setting is to hold an All Saints' festival for children and their families on the occasion of Halloween or the Feast of All Saints. Each class designs a fundraising booth for the festival. Activities such as a ring toss, a fishing pond, "guess your weight," and so on are typical of this festival. The money raised could be sent to a favorite mission or charity. Conclude the festival with an outdoor parade in which all students dress up like their favorite saints and march around the neighborhood.

National American Indian Heritage Month (S)

Let students research the ways of Native American prayer. Plan a prayer service reverencing the earth in honor of the Native American culture using traditional symbols of cornmeal, fire, and plants. Learn which Native Americans are native to your area. Listen to a recording of traditional Native American music.

The Feast of Shichi-Go-San *(November 15) (F, S)*
On this day in Japan children go to the shrines and pray for good health and fortune. This is a great day to celebrate the child within each of us. Play a game, eat an ice cream cone, read a classic children's story. As a special treat on the feast of *Shichi-Go-San,* borrow from another Asian culture and create your own fortune cookies. Put small expressions of good luck or hope for the future inside cone-shaped salty treats or tie your fortunes to a cookie.

Thanksgiving

Thanksgiving originated at a time when the spiritual dimension of life was an integral part of people's lives. Eighteenth-century Puritan society was centered in a deep, abiding faith in God. These "pilgrim people" of America found it natural to give thanks to God for all their blessings.

Thanksgiving still offers a great opportunity to reflect on all that God has done for us and to give thanks to God in recognition of that goodness and providence. On Thanksgiving we integrate the great blessings of our lives with the source of life, our Creator. We can take an ordinary "Turkey Day" and weave a simple message of the sacred throughout the celebration.

The Five Kernels of Corn (F, S)
Shortly before Thanksgiving, plan a meal for the class or for family and friends. Share the story of the first Thanksgiving. The first year the Pilgrims spent in America was bleak. Starvation loomed over their heads like earth's greatest darkness. The daily ration throughout that first winter is said to have been five kernels of corn per meal. It is no wonder that their hearts were so grateful at the second year's bountiful harvest.

Invite your guests to the table, which has been decorated for a feast. Before you bring the food to the table, bring to each hungry diner a plate with five kernels of corn (use canned or frozen corn). Let everyone eat their portions, then ask if they feel satisfied with the "meal." Discuss the empty feeling after such a meager meal.

Expand the discussion to include questions such as these: What would we do if there were no more food? What might real hunger feel like? Where in our world, our country, our city do families leave their table hungry? Show some photographs of the victims of hunger. Conclude by reflecting on the bounty we have.

After the experience of hunger has settled in their souls, serve a simple meal to your guests. As they share the meal, ask again how they feel. End this meal with a mutual prayer of thanksgiving. Ask each person for a brief prayer of gratitude, such as, "For the hands that prepared this food…." Ask everyone to respond, "We thank you, Lord."

If you are doing this activity in the classroom, you might plan a simple project to conclude your meal. Cut a 4" x 4" square of colored netting. Put five kernels of unpopped popcorn in the middle and tie with colored yarn or ribbon. Let the children each make enough for the guests at their family Thanksgiving meal. Instruct the children to place these party favors on each guest's empty plate before the family feast begins and share the story of the first winter in Plymouth with their guests.

Sharing the Bounty (F, S)

Provide a complete Thanksgiving meal for a needy family. If you are aware of a family that is unable to prepare the meal, cook, and deliver a meal for them before your own feast.

Collect canned goods and nonperishable items and take them to a local shelter for the homeless.

Spend Thanksgiving Day working in a soup kitchen. The experience of giving away your time and energy on this feast will provide food for your spirit.

A geography class might want to adopt a missionary church in a developing country. Use a map of a country to locate the mission. Your diocesan mission office will be happy to supply you with a contact in the mission church. Write to the pastor or coordinator and ask what your class could do for them. Work with all your energy to fulfill their request and pray for your special people every day. Send your donations around the time of Thanksgiving and continue to serve this mission community throughout the remainder of the year.

Fasting Before the Feast (F, S)

In the days before Thanksgiving set aside one day to fast. Plan your "famine" for a day when everyone can participate. Agree on some way as a family to deny yourselves for this one day. For example, each person could eat only a bowl of rice for dinner. Before you eat this meal offer a prayer for those who are dying of starvation. Let it be a day of reflection and prayer for those without the food gifts we take for granted.

You might want to invite a group of families to join you in this effort. On the designated day, each family can abstain and fast during the day and then gather in the evening for a simple shared meal, perhaps a meatless soup with bread. Allow the group to savor this time and share their reflections of their fasting day. End the evening with prayer. Invite each family to contribute to the prayer time with prayers of thanksgiving, readings from Scripture, stories from their own family history of days of plenty and days of want, and so on.

In the classroom this planned famine could be a lunchtime experience. Study what children in developing countries eat for their lunch (or, more realistically, for their one daily meal!). Serve this menu in the school cafeteria. It might consist of rice and water, or thin chicken broth with a few sliced carrots. After the meal is served, pass a basket to collect the money the students usually spend on dessert and snacks. Send this contribution to your school's favorite mission project.

Giving Thanks (F)

Thanksgiving is a good time for people to express their gratitude. Classes could do this on the last day of school before Thanksgiving; families could do this as they gather around the bird. Invite everyone to name something for which they're most thankful. The answers may surprise people, make them think and add to the prayerfulness of the celebration.

Remembering (F)

One of the most difficult aspects of grief is celebrating holidays after our beloved has died. One beautiful way to ease the grief and keep the memory alive at our Thanksgiving table is to add candles to the center of the table with a name card at the base of all those who have died in our family. Invite the person who mourns them to light their candle as the name is proclaimed, then pray silently for them.

Saints and Heroes

November 2 • All Souls

All of us mourn the death of our beloved dead. Children mourn too. Yet, it is very difficult for them to see beyond their pain and loneness. This feast is a time when the church prays for all those who are in the realm of eternal life, all the unofficial saints in our family tree.

A Collage of Holy Souls

Gather death cards and photograph of departed souls who the children mourn—grandparents, friends, classmates, and family members. Make a simple poster with the prayer, "Eternal rest grant unto them, O Lord," and paste all the pictures below. Allow this poster to remain on a prayer table throughout November.

Stained-Glass Project

The people who have gone before us are much like a stained-glass window: The light shines through each colored pane, revealing something beautiful. The witness of the holy souls gives us inspiration and encouragement. Give children a piece of colored tissue paper cut out in random sizes and shapes. Ask them to write in permanent marker the name of someone they love who has died. Attach these colored papers to a classroom window with black tape. Share with the children how each soul brought the image of God into our lives. Then, pray for these souls with the refrain, "Eternal light show unto them, O Lord."

November 9 • Dorothy Day (S)

Dorothy Day founded the Catholic Worker Movement through which she provided hospitality homes for the poor and homeless. In honor of this modern-day holy woman hold a Dorothy Day Canned Food Drive in commemoration of the day she was born. Take your offerings to a local center for the homeless.

Dirty Room Week (S)

In honor of Dorothy Day plan a "Dirty Room Week" to bring the class to a greater awareness of their own wealth and others' needs and to help them understand the gospel message in their own terms.

Ask children to clean their rooms this week (with a parent's help and approval). Tell them to go through closets, drawers, desks, and collect any usable toys and clothes to be given to the poor. Ask parents to sign a "Job Well Done" form and a release form for the objects the child wishes to donate. On the designated day, bring the items to class. Invite a member of a local charitable organization to accept your offering and share with the class the work that the organization does and the great need that exists in the community.

November 22 • Saint Cecilia

Saint Cecilia is the patron of music. On her feast day listen to some beautiful organ music. This is the occasion to gather the singers in your crowd to gather for a hymn fest. A hymn fest requires copies of your favorite hymnal and some willing voices to belt out a few of the favorites.

November 30 • Saint Andrew the Apostle
Some legends claim that soon after Jesus died, Saint Andrew made his way to Scotland and died there as a martyr. Saint Andrew is dear to the Scottish. To celebrate his feast they enjoy shortbread cookies in the shape of an *X*, commemorating the shape of the cross on which he was killed. Celebrate his day by using your favorite shortbread cookie recipe to make your very own Xs. While you are eating them ask his help with your own desire to be an evangelizing disciple.

Prayers
Prayer for the Poor (to honor Dorothy Day)
Preparation: You will need a table, a candle, and things to donate, such as money, clothing, and canned goods for the following prayer.

Hungry, tired, cold, and poor Jesus,
I want to see you in my world.
My world of comfort, and full refrigerators,
and shopping malls.
I know where you are, Jesus.
You are with the poor.
Light the candle.
You are standing with the twelve-year-old boy
who is ashamed to go to school
because his clothes are dirty and torn.
Help me to offer him clothes.
Put an article of clothing on the table.
You are standing with the single mom
who lives in an apartment without heat or electricity.
Help me pay her bill.
Put money on the table.

You are standing with the homeless man
who has not eaten in days.
help me to feed him.

Put canned goods on the table.

You are standing with a lonely, sick, old woman
who can no longer leave her house
because of fear and illness.
Help me to ease her pain.
Put a flower on the table.
Jesus, show us the way
to change our hearts
with actions and love.
Amen.

Native American Prayer Service

Preparation: You will need a bowl of cornmeal, a houseplant, and a candle on your prayer table. Also, you will need a small drum. Begin by sitting in a circle around the prayer table. One person slowly beats the drum while another lights the candle.

Reader One: Maker of the Earth,
trees, animals, and humans,
all is for your glory.
The drum beats it out
and the human beings shout it;
they dance the ancient dance
that says you are God.

The drum stops. One person stands, takes the bowl of cornmeal, and throws a little cornmeal first to the north, then to the east, south, and west in turn. The following prayers can be read between compass points or at the end of the cornmeal ritual.

Reader Two: O Great Spirit of the North,
we ask you for strength and power
to be strong and sure
when the cold uncertain wind

wants to blow us away.
O Great Spirit of the East,
we smile at you when the sun comes up.
Give light to our ways,
especially to those who will be born today.
O Great Spirit of the South,
whose warmth brings growth to our seeds,
help us to grow in your ways.
O Great Spirit of the West,
where each night the sun comes to rest,
bless us with peace.
All children stand.

Reader Three: Trees and living things
are one in your life.
We thank you for giving us the earth
and all its plants and animals.
We promise to care for them.
The drum begins to beat again very slowly. Everyone bows toward the prayer table and stays in a position of reverence until the drum stops.

A Thanksgiving Table Prayer
Giver of the Harvest and Source of Life,
we all stand together
grateful.
This year has brought us life, especially (name the new babies).
We are grateful for the circle of life, especially (mention any weddings or deaths) who have gone before us.
We have tasted the bounty of the earth, and bow our heads in praise and thanks.
In all these things we have known your hand
moving among us as keeper and protector,
provider and teacher.

We have known your ways
in the rising sun and the stars of night.
We have seen your touch in the embrace of one another.
And we are altogether grateful.
Amen.

DECEMBER

Advent

When the earth begins to sing of death, our hearts sense the stillness and we feel anxious about what is coming. Winter brings a time of deep quiet to life. Those who have lived long and well know there is nothing to fear in death. In this barren time, life is at rest. We learn that the earth and those who live on it need a time of stillness for birth to occur. For us to join nature in this stillness takes the grace of courage. As we settle into a winter pace, God's quiet searching voice can be heard. It is an Advent voice that speaks the hard truth calling us to turn around and prepare the way for a birth.

Advent calls us to be listeners, to hear our own spirit's longing and the response of a loving God. This exchange occurs in darkness, where nothing can distract us from the sound and sight of God moving in our midst. Just as Mary spoke her fiat with no understanding of what was to come, so too do we open our lives to the unknown ways of the encounter with Christ. The mystery of God among us still remains. In this dark winter solstice the presence of the incarnate Word begins, not as a blast of Easter trumpets, but as a small, singular note that is first heard in the birth cry of a winter night.

We are invited to be still and relish the Advent quiet. We learn that darkness is holy and that the night is a time for rejuvenating rest. All this is part of God's way for the earth and for its people. The natural cycle of the seasons speaks to the spiritual cycle of our lives. All parts of the country experience this time of winter rest even where the weather is not cold. The subtle changes of climate, the hibernation of plants and animals set the mood of rest and darkness. The paradox remains with us, that in the stillness comes the promise of future life. The invitation to walk into the silent rest of this season is always an invitation into growth and hope. Winter's song is filled with promise and wonder.

In our consumer-driven world Christmas begins about a month before Thanksgiving. Christmas decorations, caroling bells, twinkle-toed elves appear well in advance of the feast, so that shoppers will shop, spenders will spend, and profits will rise. Overwhelmed with the Christmas pitch, we find minimal public awareness of this waiting time called Advent.

Advent shines as the time of expectation. These four weeks before the celebrated birth feast are meant to symbolize centuries of yearning for the Messiah. Advent calls believers to rediscover the reasons for our belief in Jesus as the Christ. It is a season meant to encourage a personal and profound interior journey of waiting, a season modeled on the pregnant virgin's journey to give birth. Mary stands as a solitary figure of courageous hope in the midst of darkness. Mary, the human being, simply said, "yes!"

It is our task to retrieve this quiet season for our hearts and homes. Without walking into the loneliness of the wait, the word *Emmanuel*, "God with us," has little meaning. Children can rediscover the wealth of Advent traditions that turn their eyes away from television commercials for the latest toy fads and back to Jesus and the values of his gospel. The following suggestions for the season of Advent will keep young and old eyes centered on Jesus, the long-awaited Messiah.

The Advent Wreath (F, S)

A symbol central to our waiting time should be the Advent wreath. Classrooms, homes, and churches offer this symbol as a sign of the journey to Christmas. Traditionally, the wreath is made of evergreens, which represent the constant and eternal presence of God made manifest in Jesus Christ. The wreath is circular, reminding us that God's love is never-ending. Four candles are placed on the wreath to symbolize the four Sundays before Christmas. Since the liturgical color of the season is purple, three candles are purple (or white with purple ribbons attached). A fourth candle, to be lit on the third Sunday of Advent, can be pink (or white with a pink ribbon), as a sign to revel in the joy of the nearness of the feast. A fifth candle, white, known as the Christ candle, may be placed in the center of the wreath and lit on Christmas day. Each Sunday of Advent, light a new candle and say a simple prayer. You may want to read the Gospel or responsorial psalm from that day's liturgy. Families may want to begin a daily meal in these Advent weeks with a special prayer as they light their wreath. Morning prayer in the classroom can feature this ritual throughout the Advent period. Advent wreaths do not have to include evergreens. Here are some interesting variations:

The John the Baptist Wreath (F, S)

Fill a clay saucer or deep tray with sand (kitty litter is a good substitute if you do not live with a cat!). Place two or three rocks in the pot. Then make a miniature banner that reads "Prepare the Way of the Lord"; attach it to a small stick and place it in the pot. Place four candles in the sand.

This desert wreath reminds us of the Baptist's cry and suggests what life would be like without the water of life found in Jesus. If you live near the desert, this is a great time to visit the winter desert and recreate it in your Advent desert garden. You might arrange other desert objects such as a cactus and bones to illustrate this theme. This little desert place can entice children's imaginations and teach young and old alike to focus on water as the source of life.

In the days before Christmas, wet the sand and add evergreens to the "desert." Talk about the difference in sight, touch, and smell between the sand and the evergreens. Remind children that Jesus makes our spirits come alive just like water brings life to the desert. On Christmas Day, add a red bow as a symbol of God's love and a large white candle as a sign of Christ. With older children, you can add small shiny glass ornaments as a symbol of the light of Christ.

As you light the candles of your wreath on Christmas, say this prayer:

> God, may we be like shining ornaments reflecting the light of Jesus. May our lives mirror his love and his ways, not only this Christmas Day, but every day.

During the octave of Christmas, continue to light this centerpiece. Everyone can add ornaments for the times they reflected the love and light of Jesus by their actions. This activity is perfect for those back-to-school days after Christmas. Adding ornaments reminds students that for the church, Christmas continues well into January.

A Bread Dough Wreath (S)
This miniature Advent wreath is a great classroom activity. Make a small wreath of braided bread dough or any type of modeling clay and add four small birthday candles. Let the wreath dry to hardness. Then paint the wreath with bright green paint. These small wreaths can be taken home as reminders of the passing days of Advent.

The Advent Chain (F, S)
Make a paper chain to count the days before Christmas. As children remove links and the chain grows shorter, they can measure the nearness of the feast. An interesting twist to this project that attracts even the most sophisticated teen is the addition of a task written on the inside of each paper link. These tasks can be little things the family or class does to prepare for the feast. The tasks should be a mixture of physical and spiritual, fun activities and caring activities. For instance, "Offer the birds a message of hope today. Feed them a piece of bread or some seed," or, "Send a Christmas card to a lonely person," and so on. This chain not only marks the days but prepares our hearts for Christmas.

The Advent House (F, S)

Getting Christmas decorations out of storage and putting them up can be a great hassle for busy people. Here is an alternative for keeping the spirit of Advent in mind. On the First Sunday of Advent, put out just one small knickknack or wreath. Then each day of Advent add one more decoration. As Christmas approaches, put up the more flamboyant items such as door wreaths and pine boughs. Let everyone guess what decoration was added that day. As the house begins to sparkle with holiday signs, it will be harder to discover what could be new each day. Your space becomes a visual Advent calendar, and by Christmas the decorations are all in place without devoting hours to the effort.

In the classroom, this activity can keep students present to the academic space in a time when their pre-Christmas minds tend to wander. Each day of Advent the class could add something seasonal to the room: a poster, a prayer, a sprig of holly. Enjoy children's reactions as they discover the subtle placement of the new decoration. You might use each day's symbol as the introduction to the day's religion class. You could use Jesse tree symbols as a theme or create an alphabet of Advent symbols: A is for Advent wreath, B is for baby, C is for candle, and so on.

The Faces of Jesus (S)

In these days when we await Christ's coming, we might think about the many faces of Jesus Christ. Create a collage of pictures showing the races and cultures that show us the many faces of Jesus Christ among us today. Encourage students to watch for Christ in the faces of the people they meet. Add to your collage throughout Advent.

Christ Kindl (F, S)

Christ Kindl is a wonderful German tradition that teaches the spirit of giving in the finest gospel sense. Have everyone select the name of another member of the family or class through a secret drawing. Remind them to keep their *Christ Kindl*'s name to themselves till

Christmas Eve. All through the days of Advent, they do unseen favors for their *Christ Kindl* as they would for the Christ child: Hang up a coat, shine shoes, leave a Christmas cookie on a lunch plate, be thoughtful and caring in quiet ways, anything that shows love. On Christmas Eve (or the last day of school before the Eve) they reveal the identity of their *Christ Kindl*. This emphasizes the real experience of giving: not an exchange of material things, but rather, gifts from a caring heart.

This project is as successful with adult groups as with families and children. It becomes a great challenge to leave thoughtful notes in your person's mailbox, have a favorite pizza delivered on a Friday night, send a favorite book—all without being discovered.

The spirit of giving can take on a particular focus by adopting a needy family. You can find such a family by contacting a local social service agency or simply by keeping your ears and eyes open to those around you. A parish family suddenly overwhelmed by unemployment, illness, or death would be perfect for this activity. In a *Christ Kindl* spirit, prepare a cache of Christmas gifts for your family, a Christmas supper, or whatever they need most. You can let them know ahead of time or simply leave your gifts at their door and ring the doorbell, whichever is more appropriate.

Adopting needing families is a wonderful class project. Connecting with other children in need brings the spirit of Christmas into focus and balances the more material aspects of the holiday, helping the students achieve a proper perspective.

The Advent Game (F, S)

This waiting game spans many age groups and settings. It has been used in classrooms, families, prayer groups, and whole parish communities. More than a game, it is a journey into Christmas with the Holy Spirit, who enters into the play of holiness with us. Laughter and inspiration accompany this game as participants meet the joyful side of God in the works of the Spirit. It reminds us to savor the moments of Advent and prepare our hearts for the holy antics of an unpredictable God.

To play the Advent Game, find a basket, empty cookie jar or another container. Then reproduce (rewrite, type, or copy) the Advent activities that follow these directions. The first list is for family use and the second for classroom use. Personalize the activities in any ways that seem appropriate. The Spirit may have some particular ideas for your situation. Cut apart the activities, fold each, and place all in the container. On the first day of Advent, as you choose a piece of paper from the container, ask the Holy Spirit to help you draw closer to God this season. Try to perform your special daily task with a holy purpose and great determination! If you realize that the activity you have drawn is "just impossible" for this day, put it back, remind the Spirit of your schedule, and choose again.

Family Advent Activities (F)

- Read the Magnificat (Luke 1:46–55). Read the words as if Mary is sharing her thoughts and spirit with you in this ancient prayer. Keep the spirit of Mary with you throughout the day by keeping a symbol of her presence visible all day: a lighted blue candle at your table, a rosary in your pocket, or some other reminder.

- Wish your nose a "Merry Christmas." Prepare a saucepan of two cups of water, a cinnamon stick, orange peels, cloves, and nutmeg. Let this mixture simmer on low heat all day. Add water as necessary. As the sweet aroma fills your house, let it be a sensate prayer of praise that rises to a God who so loved the world that we received the only begotten Son.

- Write letters to people faraway who touched your life in a special way. Let them know that the memory of your relationship is still with you and that you will always be grateful for their role in your life. Wish them a blessed feast and let them know you will be thinking of them and praying for them this Christmas. Spend the rest of this day praying for these special people.

- Bake your favorite cookies. (If you're not a cook, visit your favorite bakery.) Freeze these scrumptious treats leaving out two cookies for each family member. In late afternoon or after supper serve these cookies with your favorite hot drink. As you enjoy your treats talk about your expectations for the season. What is your favorite part of the feast? With whom would you like to share it? What silly thing do you always love doing together?

- Go to a shopping mall. Sit in the midst of the holiday rush and watch the crowd. As you watch the passing shoppers, ask the Spirit to help you single out one overworked, overtired person to pray for. Put something on your refrigerator that will remind you to pray for this person throughout Advent, asking God's blessings, love, and peace this Christmas. Picture this person in your mind as you pray. Your prayers may be the greatest gift the person receives this Christmas.

- Listen to Christmas music. Pray the words as you listen. Let the words melt into your spirit and stay with you throughout the day.

- Invite a lonely neighbor or relative to your home during the week between Christmas Day and New Year's Day. Share the warmth and love of your home with someone who will be without these graced gifts during the feast. Plan a special menu, present a token gift. Attend to this project as if you were inviting Christ for dinner. Meditate today on these words: "Whatever you do for the least among you, you do for me."

- Take a "me" break. Remember that you are the beloved of God. How will this gracious lover treat you today? Is there something special you would enjoy today—walk in the quiet morning, a phone call to a distant friend, a leisurely afternoon nap? Let the Spirit treat you to a break in the hectic preparations. Realize that you need to pamper yourself a little so that you don't forget how loved you really are.

- Go for a ride tonight and view all the colorful Christmas lights. Get caught up in the wonder and delight of the spectacle. See it as if you have never viewed such wonder before. Allow the lights to shine in your soul. Feel the joyful glory they proclaim. Allow the light to brighten your own personal darkness tonight. As you get lost in the vision of colored lights, give back to God any pain or hurt you harbor in your heart.

- Eat lunch with a good friend. Enjoy this friendship as you break bread together. Remember to thank this special friend for all the relationship means to you. Bring a small gift if you wish, but mostly, just enjoy this dear one. Ask God to keep your friend well this Christmas.

- Think of someone who could use a little boost from God. Prepare a small and thoughtful gift for this person. Wrap your offering and attach a note that simply says, "The Lord made me think of you today." Don't sign it. Let your person feel amazed without any honor for yourself.

- Proclaim a desert day! Fast from noise today. Spend this day quietly in the house with no television, no radio, no telephone calls. Keep a deep peace in the house. Spend some extra time listening to God's voice in this quiet day. Let the Spirit speak to you about the weeks ahead and God's ways for the feast in your lives. Write down a few of these thoughts. Keep this journal in the place where you pray and remind yourself of this time of oasis and sanctuary amidst the clamor of holiday noise.

- Prepare a box of food for the poor in your community. Fill it with good simple food and a few extras such as a new dishcloth, a book of postage stamps, a bottle of hand lotion. As a family prepare and deliver your gift of love to a local center for the poor. In the evening, read together Matthew 25:31–45. Do something useless but fun! Watch or read a version of Charles Dickens's *A Christmas Carol*, make gingerbread people, build a fire, listen to Handel's *Messiah*. Do something that enriches your soul and nourishes your spirit. Waste a little time with the Lord, who loves your play as well as your work.

- Send Christmas cards to three people who wait for the mail to come to fill their day, for example, someone elderly or sick or far from loved ones. Be sure to include a little message of love with your name. Pray for these three this Advent day.

- Decorate your front door. Let the world know that they are welcome in your house and that the birth of Christ is celebrated here. As you put up your door symbol, meditate on ways your household might be more hospitable to neighbors, friends, and family. What are the things that stop you from opening your heart and home to others?
- Share this day with a child. Take your young one to a Christmas place, perhaps a public crèche or a Christmas display. Help the child make or buy a gift for a loved one. Wrap this treasure and remind your child not to tell what's in it. Share a meal together or a special treat. End the time by sharing a book about Jesus' birth. (You might want to give the child the book as a memento of the day.) Listen well to your little one today; the Spirit often speaks through such innocence.
- Take a walk at night. Listen to the sounds of night. Allow the darkness to surround you. See the walk through the darkness as an opportunity to meet God. Think about Mary and Joseph and their walk into the darkness of unknown Bethlehem. What unknown "Bethlehems" do you face in the future? As you walk, turn these unknowns over to God, just as Mary and Joseph did. End your walk by joining the song of praise of God's night creatures—the crickets and owls, the traffic and the sirens. Hear their noises as a hymn to Emmanuel.
- Cook a casserole or basket of muffins for someone with too much to do and not enough time to do it. Drop it off with an offer to help in any way you can. They will feel so good to know that you cared enough to offer.
- Bring some living greenery (pine boughs or holly, a winter flower, a Christmas cactus) into your house. Look at it, smell it, touch it! Remind yourself that our ancient Christian forebears saw the color green as a sign of God's unending love and hope. Let this greenery reign among your decorations as a sign of this marvelous Lover.
- Buy a Christmas candle. Give it a prominent place in your home.

Place your Bible next to it, opened to Luke's birth narrative. On Christmas Eve and every night of the Christmas octave (the week between Christmas and New Year's Day) light this sign of God's Son among us, read the Word, and delight in the wonder of it all.

- Make a simple Christmas decoration and place it next to your bed on a table or nightstand. Next to your decoration place a book that can prepare your spirit for Christmas. Every evening read at least one page from your book and enjoy your Christmas decoration as a reminder to savor simple pleasures in this very commercial season.

- Open the doors of your heart. Give special attention, love, and prayers to all those who come to the door of your home and workplace. Greet your telephone calls with the same hospitality and love. Welcome them all with generous attention; stop what you are doing and give them your full presence. Let this simple gift of self be a witness to the love of Christ among us. Your day will be more blessed and peaceful than you could ever imagine.

- Tell the people you live with—your children, your spouse, your parents—that you love them. Try to give each one a sincere compliment during the day. Pray that each member of your family may always know your love and the love of God. Remember that often your voice and your arms express God's love.

- Go Christmas shopping. Don't go to the shopping mall. Go to some unique little shop. Maybe you can visit a favorite bookstore or neighborhood hardware store. Enjoy buying little, inexpensive things in this one spot. Be sure to wish the salesclerk a blessed Christmas.

- Put up your crèche, but do not put the Christ child in it yet. On Christmas Eve place the babe in the manger and read the story of Christ's birth to those with whom you share this holy night.

- Make or buy holiday breads. Wrap them and deliver them to friends or neighbors. Before you deliver them, ask the Lord to bless these breads and bestow his deep and abiding presence on all those who share this bread.

- Ask forgiveness of someone you have hurt. Call or write, do whatever you must to make peace. If nothing comes to mind, ask the Lord to lead you to someone who needs your listening and understanding this Advent day.

Classroom Advent Activities (S)
Adaptable for primary through junior high students.

- Read the story of the Annunciation (Luke 1:26–56). Act out the story as a play for another class. How do you think Mary felt when she said the words of the Magnificat? List words that describe how Mary might have felt after her visit from the angel.
- Wish your nose a Merry Christmas. Bring something to class tomorrow that has a "Christmas smell"—a piece of pine bough, a cinnamon stick, an orange peel, a candle—whatever smells like Christmas to you. Share your smells with one another and tell about a memory connected with this smell. Write a "Thank you for my Christmas nose" prayer.
- Give your students this assignment: Write letters to people who have helped you grow and learn. Include in your letters how important these people are to you. End with a prayer for their happiness and peace this Christmas. Send these letters to these special people as a Christmas surprise.
- Plan a Christmas cookie party. Have everyone bring four to six Christmas cookies to class. Put all the cookies on a large platter and enjoy this treat at the end of the school day. After you all have finished, give thanks to God for all the wonder and fun of these holy days.
- Listen to a Christmas carol and learn all the words. Pick a carol that most people have never learned or the second and third verses of a popular Christmas song. When students go home, ask them to sing it for their family.
- Get the name and address of a homebound person in your parish or community. Make a Christmas card for this person and have stu-

dents write a cheerful note inside. Send a few each week until Christmas. Perhaps one or more people in your class can visit this person during the week between Christmas and New Year's Day.

- Assign writing down the name of a person students know who could use God's loving help and prayers. This person might be a sick relative, an overworked mom, a friend who has a problem, a famous person. Put all the papers in a basket. Have each student pick one and tape it to the corner of their desk as a reminder to say a special prayer for this person each day until Christmas.

- Talk about the meaning of light in our Christian tradition. Ask students: Why do we put lights all over the Christmas tree? For homework tonight find out when and where the tradition of putting lights on Christmas trees began and why we do this.

- Assign an essay about a good friend who lives far away. Tell the class what makes this person such a special friend. Then assign writing a short Christmas letter to this person and include a copy of the essay.

- Put the names of everyone in the class in a basket. Take a name from the basket. Be sure students don't get their own name. Have each person do something nice for the picked name today, but keep it secret. When they discover that another has done something nice for them today, believe that this good deed was a special touch of God's hand.

- This is a day to fast. Decide on some way of fasting or doing without: Ask the students to not talk in the halls, or not buy sugary treats in the cafeteria, or give up a recess to perform some useful task for the school. Whatever they decide, have them do it with a quiet love for the Lord who is coming so soon.

- Bring in some food for the poor. Collect a box of canned goods and boxed foods for the poor in the community. Be sure to include some fun items in the food box, such as jars of jelly and nice-smelling soaps.

- Do something fun and useless. Have an unscheduled art project, see a Christmas movie, work a crossword puzzle, have a Christmas spelling bee (using only seasonal words). Have fun together with no real purpose in mind.
- Create a Christmas card for students' parent(s). Be sure to have them write "I love you" and offer wishes for the best Christmas ever!
- Decorate your classroom door. Draw outlines of your hands on green construction paper, cut them out, and write the names of students on them with red crayon. With the fingers pointed down, build a tree-shaped pyramid of your green hands. On the very top, place a bright yellow star with the name of your class on it.
- Encourage students to spend some time with a younger brother or sister (if they don't have one, spend time with a friend's brother or sister). Tell them to read a story, play a game, go for a walk. For homework tonight, they should write about what they did with this younger person and how they feel about the time spent together.
- As a class, go to a darkened room. Sit together in the quiet dark space in absolute silence. Then light one bright candle. Watch how the candle fills the room with beautiful light. Listen to the carol "Silent Night." Really listen to the words as you watch the candle. Remember in your heart how the darkness felt and how the light felt. Remember that Jesus came to bring light to all of us and put away the darkness forever.
- For homework, assign writing down a favorite Christmas recipe students always share at their homes—a Yule log cake, a Christmas salad, Aunt June's cookies, whatever. Have each student share the recipes with the class and tell why it is so special. If you are really ambitious, put all your students recipes together to create your own class Christmas cookbook as a surprise gift for parents this Christmas.
- Bring to class some living plant that stays green all winter—a pine bough, a sprig of holly, an evergreen branch. Notice the wonderful

smells of these winter greens. Ask students: How is God's love like these green plants?

- Ask students to bring old Christmas cards to school. Ask them to design a small poster. Include a catchy slogan and lots of artwork. Use this poster to remind the class that the real reason we celebrate Christmas is not because we get a lot of gifts, but because Jesus became one of us. Vote on the best poster. Encourage students to take the creation home and put it next to their bed.

- Assign an essay about being a giver instead of a getter. Ask students: If you could give each person in your family one special gift of love, what would it be? Ask them to write about what would truly make the people in their families happy this Christmas.

- Ask your class to find out how the nativity scene or crèche first came into use. Have each student share with the class what their favorite nativity scene looks like. Do they have one at home? Have they ever visited a large, outdoor version? Why do you think people enjoy looking at these scenes?

Christmas

Hodie Christus natus est! Christ is born today! We do not know if Jesus was born on the twenty-fifth of December, but the historical accuracy of this date is not nearly as important as what we do know, which is that Jesus the Christ took on human form, lived among us, and calls us back to God as he invites us to live his gospel. This knowledge is what we celebrate at Christmas. Yet to celebrate on this date is no accident. The early church chose to link the birth of Jesus with the pagan feast of the winter solstice. Early Christian thinkers infused new meaning into winter's darkness by declaring the darkest time of the year as the occasion of the birth of the new and eternal light. Earth and heaven merge in a new reality.

With the first bells of midnight the fun begins. It is time to enjoy the preparations of heart and home with joy. Relax and enter into the wonder and fun of the day. Before you decide to do any of the activities suggested here, ask, "Does this activity enhance or hinder the Christ-life among us?" "Will the event bring us joy, or is it just one more thing to get done before Christmas?" Be selective about how you choose to celebrate. Give your schedule plenty of time for quiet. This is meant to be a season of joyful reflection. Allow for a generous amount of reflective time or all your busy days will be wasted.

This day can be as joyous or horrendous as you allow it to be. Christmas turns into an overwhelming, exhausting experience in so many households because we overdo the celebration. We want to put every happy moment, every perfect gift, every loving moment into a day that just can't hold it all. In the process, we manage to crowd out the cause of the feast. I strongly recommend that you look at this day in a defensive way. Do battle against wanting too much, spending too much, even loving too much. Plan the feast well in advance. Leave ample time to relax and enjoy the company, the food, the gifts. Keep all these things simple.

We expect Christmas to be perfect, but in reality our homes are not like those in the magazines, we are not as handsome as the models in the commercials, and our tables don't look like the ones pictured in the gourmet cookbooks. Don't try to measure up to such standards. Keep Christmas in your hearts. Jesus wants to shine in a sanctuary of family love, not a picture-perfect scenario of a television holiday special. Be who you are on Christmas Day and enjoy the simple fun and profound meaning of the feast.

These suggestions offer a variety of ways to enter the feast of Christmas. Look at them with a sense of what fits your soul and how you can ritualize the journey to the manger. Let the rituals and symbols of Christmas be particular to your needs in the classroom and in the family.

Collecting Memories (F, S)

As we look back on our own childhood Christmas memories, it is not the gifts received that we remember, but rather, the good times, the funny moments, the poignant events that stay with us. We retain little memory of how clean the house was or the menu of the day. What remains are the moments of love and joy: when Dad gave Mom his heartfelt gift and she cried; when Uncle Ed's chair broke in the middle of Christmas dinner; when little Billy sang a carol in the dark of his room when everyone thought he was sleeping. These moments become the treasures of Christmas past.

It is important for families to preserve and retell the memories of the past. As we revere our past we proclaim our history as the church, the family, the people who are loved. We say to ourselves and to our children, "This is who we are. We are lovable and unique. We have been given great gifts." Christmas is a feast filled with such memory moments. As we nurture our children, it is important to share with them our family stories. The following are a few ways to preserve the memories of Christmas past.

An Ornament Collection (F)

Each year make or buy an ornament for your child. Date the ornament and attach a small tag to it. On the tag, write something quotable the child said. For example, you might record what the child said when opening a favorite gift. This collection of ornaments plus any others they make or receive in the childhood years should be collected in a special storage box. You might want to add unique personal items to the hanging collection, such as a baby rattle, a favorite piece of jewelry, or a small picture in a hanging frame. When the child leaves your household, you can present this box of memories with your best wishes as he or she begins a new phase of life.

The Family Ornament (F)

Each year make or buy a family ornament. Ornaments could be symbols of something important or memorable that happened since last Christmas—a vacation memento, a photograph of a loved one who achieved something special—or who died and achieved salvation! These small tokens will remind you of family stories. Be sure that every family member gets in the act of designing this ornament. Put aside some family time before Christmas to assemble your project. Make a tag for it with everyone's name and age and the date. Each year when you pull it from its storage box, you will remember the fun and joy that went into making it. Long after the days of family ornament projects, your tree will bring you the delight of little hands and helpful hearts that have grown up and gone on with their own Christmas.

The Class Ornament (S)

Every teacher knows that each class is a unique blend of character and spirit. Suggest an activity before Christmas that lets students know how special they are. Design a class ornament that tells the story of who these children are as a class. Their symbol could tell about an event or honor they share, or it could commemorate an event that occurred in their school year. Just be sure it is like no other design. Put this new ornament on the class or school Christmas tree with those of past classes. Over the years through your teaching journey, the tree will chronicle for your students the history of your experiences as a teacher. Children will enjoy hearing about your other school Christmases. If you are in midstream in your teaching career, make some past-year ornaments from old photographs and gifts that you have collected. This is a perfect way to show off those handmade treasures that every teacher receives from generous hearts over the years.

Book/DVD Collections (F, S)

Both in the family and in the classroom, children's literature plays an important role in developing imagination, creativity, and values. The great treasure of children's Christmas literature provides a wonderful source of inspiration as a child awaits the feast.

Each year acquire a book that tells the Christmas story in a new way. Two classics are O. Henry's story "The Gift of the Magi" or Charles Dickens's *A Christmas Carol*. On the inside cover, write the date and the names and ages of the children who will share the book. Begin this collection and watch the delight in your children's eyes as these treasured books resurface to be enjoyed for another year. These books become the old friends of Christmas. Be sure to display your collection only between Christmas and New Year's and then pack them away till next year's visit. The book's inside cover is a great place to write your memories of each year's feast. The collection becomes a treasured display of memories as well as a valuable and fun resource.

A twist to this collection is to compile a DVD library of Christmas TV and cartoon specials and classic holiday films. You may want to restrict viewing time during the Christmas octave between Christmas and New Year by featuring a "special" film or cartoon each evening.

This is a delightful way to mark the family's growth. Your first books and cartoons will appeal to toddlers. As children mature the family Christmas library will include classics.

The classroom Christmas library takes on the added value of offering students an opportunity to integrate literature into the hectic, pre-Christmas curriculum. One story or chapter could be used each day as the thematic center of many subject areas: Discuss the book as part of religion class, plan a reading or grammar lesson using the book, give a writing assignment related to it, or even incorporate it into a science, geography, or history class.

You might want to let the students earn the funds to purchase their class Christmas book each year. Begin collecting nickels and dimes as soon as school begins so that your December purchase is well-funded. Inscribe all the students' names on the inside of the book. The book could be donated to a permanent collection in the school library as their Christmas gift to their school.

A Christmas Album (F, S)

Photographs of special moments preserve stories of love and laughter and bring these moments to life again. These moments remembered and shared in pictures help build self-esteem. They say: This is my story. This is why I love and am loved. Christmas is a perfect time to celebrate love, to strengthen and uphold our family image, and reaffirm our origins of love.

Start a Christmas album. Fill the pages with memories of past Christmases, pictures of each holiday year, favorite notes, and cards. Every year add new pages. Write about how you spent the season, favorite gifts given and received, and touching moments. Place this album in a prominent place for everyone to enjoy. You will notice family members sneaking away with the album for a quiet reverie with their memories. The presence of this album and the reminders it offers can quell preseason stress as family members are reminded in pictures and words that their lives are rooted in love.

A video record is another great technique to mark Christmas past. If you own a video camera, use it to record the lighting of the Advent wreath, putting up decorations, baking Christmas cookies, greetings from visiting loved ones, and so on. Create a new tape for each year. You could include interviews with older members of your family asking them to share their fondest, funniest, even saddest Christmases.

In the classroom a Christmas album can reinforce the unique character of each class and be a real curiosity as students look back on their predecessors. Take a class photograph. Write about special school activities and projects in which the class participated. The fun of forming a special class identity in this album boosts the class's self-esteem and lets them know in a subtle way how lovable they are!

Another approach to this project is to make individual albums for the students. Let each student fill an album with pictures, Christmas essays, prayers, poetry, and mementos. This holiday project is a perfect gift for parents.

A Collection of Toys (F, S)

Toys are not just for the young. We all need to remember how to play. At Christmas, when we celebrate the birth and childhood of Jesus, we celebrate not only the children among us but also the child within us. Receiving and giving toys is a delightful way to do this. Start a collection of Christmas toys. Each year acquire one new toy that belongs to everyone who sits beneath your tree to play. You might add old and treasured toys to this collection. If you're creative, you might want to make some of the toys. Grandparents especially enjoy this activity. Notice how visitors react when they play with the toys beneath your tree. They will begin to arrive each year in joyful expectation of being able to play with your toys. When the Christmas season ends, put away your toys till next year.

In the classroom you might give students an opportunity to share some favorite playthings. Assign each child a separate day to bring a favorite toy to school. Allow time to share toys. Plan this activity before Christmas to help children assess what toys mean to them. Is it the latest fad toy that becomes their favorite? What is it that makes a toy enjoyable? Why do some toys lose their attraction soon after they are received? This exercise can balance the barrage of consumer advertising that overwhelms children in these pre-Christmas days.

A Tablecloth of Memories (F)

Purchase a plain white tablecloth and a collection of permanent felt tip pens in a variety of colors. Put this tablecloth on your table each Christmas. You may want to put several layers of absorbent paper or heavy plastic beneath it. As guests arrive at your home during Christmas, invite them to autograph your tablecloth, write a special message, or draw a Christmas doodle. As years pass and the tablecloth reappears on the Christmas table, it tells a story of how you celebrate Christmas in your home. Signatures of old friends and saints grace your table years after they first came into your Christmas.

Handmade Gifts and Cards (F, S)

A handmade gift is a great treasure. The intangible qualities of another's work and love are priceless. Plan an activity for your family or class in which they make a gift for someone. Keep the project simple. Plan these projects well in advance of December and collect all the needed materials. Little ones could paint rocks that become paperweights for Grandpa and Grandma. Popsicle stick trivets are a favorite project for primary students. Older children can weave placemats, design coupons for chores and surprises such as back rubs, babysitting, or cleaning the garage.

Set a date in early December for your gift-making day. If you're doing this as a family, be sure to involve everyone. Watch the delight and excitement as family members become engrossed in this activity. As the family or class works together, they learn a valuable lesson about Christmas: It is not what you give as much as how you give. After finishing projects, share a special holiday snack. Christmas cookies and eggnog, cocoa, or hot cider serve as fitting reward for an evening of love and labor in the true spirit of Christmas giving.

Another possibility is to make your own Christmas cards. Create designs with stencils or stamps, or draw a design with black marker and reproduce it on a copier. In the classroom children can illustrate their Christmas cards and give them as gifts to Mom and Dad. Children's artwork never fails to express new insights into our more sophisticated images of the feast.

Christmas Card Writing Party (F, S)

Invite friends and family together or spend a class period with the purpose of sending Christmas cards to anyone who is in need of your thoughts and presence this Christmas. Send cards to the poor and lonely, to politicians, to old friends, and strangers. Let the card tell of your love for them this Christmas.

Créche-Making (F)

Saint Francis gave us the nativity scene. In Italian homes the family creates a crèche each Advent to display throughout the octave of Christmas. The crèche is burned at the end of the feast. This year, design your own crèche. Give each person modeling clay, white soap, or soft wood and ask them to create one figure for the scene. Put it all together on Christmas Eve.

Sharing Christmas With Sister Bird and Brother Squirrel (F, S)

It is a custom on many farms to leave a small portion of the crop unharvested as a gift to the creatures with whom we share the earth. In these barren winter days it is good for our souls to celebrate our kinship with all of creation by offering a Christmas treat to wild creatures. Near the feast of Christmas leave a tray of seed, corn, and nuts for the birds and animals that surround you. Offer this gift on Christmas morning and invite all the creatures of the land and air to join you in a hymn of praise to the newborn Messiah. As the birds come to share the feast, enjoy the first moments of your Christmas as moments of giving. Listen to the sounds of nature that welcome your gift.

In adapting this for the classroom collect enough pinecones for all students. Tie pieces of strong cord to the pinecones, then smear them with peanut butter and roll them in a bowl of birdseed. Let students hang their gooey gifts on trees on the school grounds. These birdseed ornaments become a delicious treat for the local winged population.

As long as you are knee-deep in birdseed and peanut butter, you might want to let students make an extra pinecone treat to take home for their yards. This project also makes an excellent gift for someone who is homebound and can view the birdie treat from indoors.

A less messy activity is to put unsalted peanuts in the shell on your windowsill and watch Brother Squirrel enjoy a winter feast!

The Music of Christmas (F, S)

Music often lifts us beyond the mundane into the realm of the spirit. Christmas carols not only remind us of the meaning of the feast, but the melodies fill our hearts with the memories, the feelings, the experience of Christmas. It is fitting to stop our busy preparations from time to time to savor the holy songs of the feast. These activities encourage hearing Christmas carols as prayer:

Learn the story behind one of the traditional carols. Listen to all the verses of the carol as if you were praying the words.

Attend a Christmas concert as a class or family. Make this event a special time together.

Gather the family or class around your CD player or piano to sing Christmas songs with gusto. Invite others to your Christmas sing along and enjoy the fun of remembering all the verses and harmonizing the easy parts! If you have a video camera, you might want to make a permanent record of the fun. Afterward, reward yourselves with some special holiday treats.

Listen to a new Christmas recording. You can purchase one or borrow one from the public library or exchange music favorites with friends, neighbors, or other teachers. Choose something you've never heard before. It is particularly enjoyable to gather in the dark and light the room with only the lights of the tree and a Christmas candle. Ask everyone to get comfortable and sit in stillness for a short time. Begin the recording and savor the sound with reverence.

Go caroling in your neighborhood and even turn your caroling journey into a progressive supper: At the first house eat Christmas hors d'oeuvres. Carol to the second house, where you share a salad, and at the third house meet for a hearty soup or stew. Carol to the fourth house where a well-deserved dessert awaits. If you have the appetite for this adventure but not the voice, you can bring along a portable CD or MP3 player as backup support for this night of music.

Another caroling option is to take your troupe to a nursing home or hospital. You can even carol for homebound or elderly parishioners.

The Feast of Lights (F, S)

The use of light as a symbol of God's presence is most magnificent in the Christmas season. This holiday gives all of us an opportunity to understand the image of light as a wordless expression of God among us. Here are a few ideas that can encourage that understanding:

Go for a ride on the nights before Christmas and visit the most notable light displays in your community. The dazzle and sparkle will awaken childlike wonder.

Prepare a Christmas candle for your family or class. It can be simple or fancy. Place it next to the crèche. On the eve of Christmas or the last day of school, light your candle. Remind everyone that the candle is a sign of the presence of Jesus in your midst. Burn the candle throughout the Christmas season whenever you gather together.

Plan a "tree picnic" for the day you put up your Christmas tree. Spread a tablecloth beneath the tree and serve a picnic meal of casual and simple food. Eat beneath the lights of your tree. Spend the mealtime talking about the meaning of the tree lights and remembering the significance and origin of your favorite ornaments. This picnic can end with the reading of a favorite Christmas story or poem. Let the night be devoid of television, cell phones, MP3s, handheld video games, and so on. Entertain one another with your conversation and laughter.

Celebrating Christmas Eve (F)

Christian families often have traditions for this night. Some serve special menus, some open one gift, some open all their gifts, some worship together on this holy night, some invite special guests. Whatever your customs, try to keep this night sacred, to reflect on the mystery of Incarnation. You *can* celebrate a Christmas Eve that encourages this sense of the sacred in our midst.

In many cultures Christmas Eve is a day for fasting. In Poland, for example, people abstain and fast till the first star appears in the night sky. As soon as children see the star, a great feast is spread on the table and the fast is broken to celebrate with joy the appearance of the savior's birth star. Begin a similar custom in your home. Spend the day fasting. Watch for the first star of Christmas; when it appears, remove the Advent wreath, replace it with the Christmas candle, and serve a feast of love.

Hide the infant Jesus of your crèche scene. Ask children in your house to search for the hidden infant. Remind them that just as the Hebrews looked for the Messiah, so too must they search. Whoever finds the baby Jesus places him in the manger as the Christmas candle is lit.

Plan a family prayer service for this night. Include the readings for the feast of Christmas. Ask everyone in the family to share a personal prayer at this time. End this prayer time with a period of silence so everyone can become aware of the presence of Christ in their midst. Close with a simple carol or hymn.

Walk at night and watch Christmas unfold in the houses you pass. Listen to the sounds of the season of this joyful night. Be aware of the full spectrum of life around you. Pray for the people you pass. Praise the newborn Christ with the night creatures, the moon, and stars. When you arrive home, share your reflections with one another. What homes seemed most joyful as you passed? What saddened you on this walk? When did you begin to feel the celebration of the feast? What gift did you receive on this night walk?

Bake a birthday cake for Jesus. Prepare a Christmas cake fit for a king and plan to serve it as the evening wanes and bedtimes approach. Start a procession of children bringing the cake to the manger. Sing "Happy Birthday" to Jesus, and a variety of carols. Little ones delight in this ritual because in the cake and candles they really understand the reason for our happiness.

Beginning Christmas Day (F)

Begin Christmas Day with a simple family prayer of praise in the morning darkness. Then light the Christmas candle. You might want to give each family member a candle to light from this one candle. The family then processes to candles positioned throughout the house, lighting them and singing a carol or listening to Christmas music. The candles should be allowed to burn throughout Christmas day as a symbol that the light is with us and we are filled with delight. (Caution is necessary! Children should not be left unattended with burning candles, nor should candles be left burning in empty rooms.)

Opening Family Gifts (F)

Some families open gifts on Christmas Eve, some on Christmas Day. Some buy many gifts, some a few. Some wrap them, some simply place them beneath the tree. All this is a matter of style, tradition, and preference. What remains as the important issue is that these gifts *never* replace the Lord as the cause for the feast.

Do whatever you must to keep gift-giving in proper perspective. Do not allow the consumer message that "things bring happiness" to influence the beautiful ritual of giving simply with love. As you purchase and make your offerings, keep in mind that these presents are meant to be symbols of your love for one another. They are meant to reinforce the generosity you feel for those you love. Set a limit to what you spend on these gifts and stick to it. Try to be mindful of family members with tighter budgets than yours. The gift says, "I am giving you my heart today." On Christmas the tokens of love we exchange should be shining symbols of the love that began in Jesus in the first birth cry.

Guidelines for Christmas Giving (F)

- Only one person at a time opens a gift while everyone else watches and enjoys the opening. After every person present has opened one gift, hold a short recess (perhaps ten minutes) while the receivers and givers can savor the gifts and the thoughts that went into the choices.
- Make as many gifts as possible. Handmade gifts are more valuable in the ways of the spirit than store-bought things. A hand-knit sweater, a Christmas poem, a painted rock paperweight, a woven pot holder, a wooden toy—the list goes on and on. Start planning early and try to simplify what you give.
- Wrap your gifts in recycled paper, old Sunday comic paper, reusable bags. Be conscious of the need to conserve. Reuse Christmas wrap and trimmings whenever possible.
- Extended families who exchange names for gift-giving might try a yearly theme. For example, one year all the gifts could come from a yard sale or thrift store. The next year the theme could be crazy sweatshirts and T-shirts or perhaps subscriptions to obscure and interesting magazines. Another suggestion is to purchase tickets to an event that everyone attends together. This method of directing

the gift-giving keeps things in proportion. It is hilarious fun to open the wild and strange things that result from this creative shopping invitation. It is important to exchange names very early. Whether you decide on a theme for giving or just use your imagination, this process takes some thought, time, and effort, but it's well worth it.

• Give everyone at least one toy. Toys invite play. On this feast we need to relax with one another and play together. The child within needs to be honored on this day. Laughter, playful challenges, and friendly competition allow the child in each of us to flourish. All too soon adults must return to their responsibilities. Let Christmas be a time of play.

Giving a Gift to Jesus (F)

How strange it is that Jesus does not receive presents on Christmas! We open piles of Christmas bundles with little thought to giving a gift to Jesus. Little children love to prepare such a gift for the Lord. Ask everyone in the family to prepare a gift for Jesus. Young children can present him with a favorite toy; older children can offer the Lord a special pledge or project. These gifts for Jesus should be opened before any personal family gifts. Encourage the entire family to be serious about their Jesus gift. Put these offerings around the crèche scene throughout the Christmas season as a reminder of your intention.

More December Celebrations
Hanukkah (F)

The Jewish Festival of Lights is celebrated about the same time as Christmas. Check a calendar for the date each year. Research this feast or invite a Jewish friend or relative to your classroom or home to explain its rituals. Be sure to find out about Judah Maccabee. Create your own menorah, a special candleholder with eight candles, one for each night of Hanukkah. Light one candle each night of the eight-day feast.

Kwanzaa (December 26) (F, S)

Kwanzaa is a family observance that begins on this day in recognition of the African harvest festivals. *Kwanzaa* means "first fruit" in Swahili. Kwanzaa is a celebration of family and values that begins on December 26 and continues till January 1. The seven principles, or *Nguzo Saba*, are featured during the week, one each day. The seven principles are: unity, self-determination, collective work, cooperative economics, purpose, creativity, and faith. Each day of Kwanzaa a red, green, or black candle is lit and the family reflects on the principle of the day. Cultural and historical gifts are exchanged to enhance the meaning of the day's principle. These universal values align well with the values of Catholic education.

In the classroom several students could explore the history of Kwanzaa and its originator, Dr. Maulana Karenga.

Festival of Tachiu (December 27) (F)

The festival of Tachiu is a Taoist celebration in Hong Kong. It is a day set aside for peace and renewal. Enjoy a little renewal in this busy month. Plan to set aside time this day for a quiet walk, a good book, or a long nap.

New Year's Eve (December 31) (F)

On New Year's Eve bells will ring everywhere to announce the first day of the New Year. Bells are a symbol of gathering God's people. We see them on Christmas cards and invitations. Bells ring bringing us into God's presence.

Make bells the focus of your evening celebration. Serve bell-shaped cookies and cakes. Ask your guests to bring a bell to the gathering to ring with joy at midnight. If you plan a quiet alone evening on this night, enjoy the sound of a bells as you call yourself to prayer. In this next year use your bell to open each time of prayer. Let this sound be the voice of God's invitation to come to him and listen. When you are out and about become more mindful of the sound of ringing bells.

Connection: Find a bell to use at your prayer table this next year.

Holy Family

The Feast of the Holy Family is ordinarily celebrated on the Sunday between Christmas and New Year's Day. We celebrate the reality that Jesus, just like the rest of us, came from a family. Like us, Jesus came from a family full of history. His ancestors were kings and beggars, prophets and fools. His family lived modestly and was not what we would call today, "upwardly mobile." Most notably, his mother was pregnant with him before she married Joseph.

In this simple feast we also celebrate the wonder of family life. Family is the place where each of us—student, grandparent, mom, dad—is nurtured. Jesus' family life allowed him to grow into the vision the Father held up for him. The daily witness of Mary and Joseph in Jesus' early years helped him to understand the power of love. It is no different for each of us. This is what we celebrate in this feast. The power of love given and received in the family becomes the church's focus as we look to the life of Jesus and how his story becomes our own.

Family Night Party (F)

Invite as many family members as possible. Serve foods that represent the ethnic background of the family. Ask each person present to share a memory of a family event that is either humorous or poignant or simply says, "This is who we are." If you can remember old stories that you heard from grandparents or others about the early days of your family, share them in addition to the more recent memories. Recording these wonderful stories would make the evening a permanent memory. This record could be reproduced and given to new members of the family as a wedding gift.

Building Together on Joseph Saturday (F)
On the Saturday before the Feast of the Holy Family, get out the hammers, nails, drills, and saws. Repair, sand, and clean anything wooden in your house. Put the leg back on an old chair, repair the basement door, and rehang the bookshelves. Do it all in honor of Joseph. Just as the ultimate father-and-son team must have enjoyed their work together, your family can take this opportunity to work together. (This activity is also a great project for the feasts of Saint Joseph, March 19, and Saint Joseph the Worker, May 1.)

Family Album (F)
Construct a family album. Let family members list the dates of their sacraments, important achievements, and humorous anecdotes. Include important pictures and newspaper clippings. Try to go back as far as possible into the family tree. Each year on this feast of the Holy Family add the latest data to this treasured book.

Celebrate the Family
Since schools are closed between Christmas and New Year's Day, these activities are perfect for back-to-school projects.

Family Tree (S)
Spend some time discussing Jesus' family tree. Discover why he was called the "Son of David." Do family tree projects with the class. Ask children to include the religion of each of their ancestors in addition to the usual information.

Understanding Where We Come From (S)
Help children discover how the unique blend of heritage, religion, and ethnicity makes them the special people they are. Read together some children's stories that discuss Jesus' family life. Ask children to write their own stories about a day in the life of Jesus when he was their age.

Family Photo Project (S)
Ask children to bring in photos of favorite family members. Hang the pictures together in a prominent area. Throughout the week, ask each child to tell a favorite story about the person in the picture.

Saints and Heroes
December 2 • Isaiah (F, S)
This is a day to celebrate Isaiah the prophet. Isaiah and John the Baptist are the great saints of Advent. Read Isaiah 43: "I have called you by name, you are mine." Make a list of the names God calls you. Then list the good names you hear about others with whom you live, work, or go to school. Tell one of them a name they may not have heard.

December 6 • Saint Nicholas (F, S)
In Holland and other European countries, this feast is celebrated by putting out a stocking or wooden shoe on the night of December fifth. The saint visits in the night and leaves treats of nuts and fruit.

This is a great time to communicate with the saint of generous love. On the night before the feast, put out a stocking or shoe and include a letter to Saint Nick. Ask children to talk to the saint about what they hope for during the feast of Christmas. The next morning the children will find goodies in the stocking and a return letter from the saint (thanks to a parental secretary!). This letter tells the child of God's great love for us and the true meaning of Christmas. It might also offer a few suggestions on how the little ones might become more saintly themselves before Christmas!

Another fun idea is to deliver secret stocking surprises to older folks, college folks and even "Scrooge" folks on the sixth of December. Prepare some Christmas stockings with treats, address them, and leave them in creative places: Aunt Pearl's mailbox, your college son's dorm room, the boss' desktop. Just like Saint Nick, do this generous deed anonymously!

December 8 • The Immaculate Conception (F)

This is Magnify the Lord Day. Join Mary in magnifying God's presence in the world today. Go to the grocery store, the shopping mall, the subway station—any scene of short tempers and hectic life. Stand in the midst of the place and offer a silent prayer of praise to God. You might recite the Gloria or your favorite praise prayer to yourself. Let the secret power of praise fill the earth.

December 10 • Thomas Merton (F, S)

Thomas Merton died on this day in 1968. Merton was a Trappist monk and spiritual leader. Celebrate his life by seeking some silent place to meet God on this day. As a group or individually, light a candle and sit with God without saying a word. Feel the presence of God within.

December 12 • Our Lady of Guadalupe (F, S)

This is a day to celebrate Our Lady with Catholics of Mexican heritage. In 1531, the virgin appeared as a young, pregnant Aztec maiden. Begin the day with the "Hail Mary." If possible recite this prayer in Spanish. Offer a toast to Our Mother with hot chocolate and sweet treats. For the really adventurous, serve *menudo*, a hot tripe soup. At this time, the gardens of western Mexico produce the first fruits of winter's bounty. With your tripe soup serve a large "Guadalupe" salad filled with Mexican delights in honor of the virgin who brought forth roses in December.

Menudo (Tripe and Hominy Soup)

Menudo is a soup of tripe and corn or hominy. It is a classic part of Christmas holiday meals in Mexico. A bowl of *menudo* is said to cure a hangover and to have other medicinal powers.

5 pounds tripe*
1/2 pound veal, cut in small pieces
1 tablespoon cooking oil
3 cloves garlic
1 tablespoon salt

1 1/2 cups chopped onion
1 teaspoon chopped cilantro
2 tablespoons chili powder
8 cups water
1 large can hominy
2 tablespoons lemon juice, chopped green onions, and cilantro or fresh mint

*2 pounds precooked pork may be substituted for the tripe. While this is not authentic *menudo*, it is more palatable for the faint of heart!

Cut tripe in 3-inch pieces. Brown the veal in the oil in a large kettle. Add tripe, garlic, salt, onion, cilantro, chili powder, and water. Cover and simmer for eight hours until the tripe is tender. Be sure to add more water when necessary. Add the hominy, heat, then add lemon juice. Serve with a garnish of green onions and cilantro or mint.

Buñuelos (Fried Sweet Puffs)
This is a favorite Mexican pastry served on Christmas Eve and other special occasions.

3 1/2 cups all-purpose flour
1 teaspoon salt
1 teaspoon baking powder
2 tablespoons sugar
1/4 cup butter or margarine
2 eggs
1/2 cup milk
oil for deep frying
confectioners' sugar

Sift flour with salt, baking powder and sugar into a bowl. Add butter with a pastry blender until it resembles coarse meal. Beat eggs and milk together and stir into dry ingredients until a ball of dough forms. Turn ball out onto a floured surface and knead for 3 minutes or until the dough is very smooth. Cut dough into grape-size pieces and let rest for 20 minutes. Roll each ball out on a flour board so that it is about 4 inches in diameter, and cut a hole in the center with a thimble. Fry in hot oil (375 degrees) until puffed and golden, about 20 seconds on each side. Drain on a paper towel and sprinkle with confectioners' sugar.

December 13 • Saint Lucy (F)

In Sweden on the feast of this saint of light the eldest daughter rises early and prepares fresh pastries for the household. She carries the breakfast to her parents' bed with a wreath of lighted candles in her hair. (Don't try this at home!) Share in this tradition with a breakfast of warm coffee cake or rolls and coffee or tea in honor of Saint Lucy. Place a lighted candle on the breakfast table.

Saint Lucy's name is derived form the Latin word *lux,* meaning "light." In the old Julian calendar (before our current Gregorian calendar) December 12 was the longest night of the year. On Saint Lucy's Day we celebrate that the inner light of Christ outshines the darkness. This is a wonderful time to record the length of daylight and give thanks for the coming of the light.

Go out into the night and look for Saint Lucy stars, the early morning/late night meteors that flash across the December skies.

December 16 • Las Posadas (F)

Tonight the Advent novena *Las Posadas* starts. The custom brings neighbors together as they leave their homes and go house to house asking for lodging in memory of Mary and Joseph in Bethlehem. This is a day to reflect on the ways of hospitality. Invite to your classroom or home someone who immigrated to this country. Ask them to share with you their experience of welcome or unwelcome here. Resolve to see strangers as wayfarers who, like the Virgin, are bearers of Jesus.

This is a wonderful time to do something for the homeless. Take a field trip to a homeless shelter and work in the kitchen. Collect soap and shampoo for a drop-in center. Send a cash donation to a center for the homeless.

December 17 • The "O's" (F, S)

Today we begin the "O" antiphons for the final days of Advent. From December 17 through December 23 we listen to the titles of Jesus that have become familiar to us through "O Come, O Come Emmanuel," the ancient Advent hymn of praise.

> December 17: "O come, O wisdom from on high"
> December 18: "O come, O come, O Lord of might"
> December 19: "O come, O flower of Jesse's stem"
> December 20: "O come, O key of David, come"
> December 21: "O come, O daystar shining bright"
> December 22: "O come, desire of the nations"
> December 23: "O come, O come Emmanuel"

To celebrate the "O's" create symbols for each of the antiphons. Make simple ornaments with these symbols to use as tree decorations. A lamp for wisdom, a rock for might, a rose for Jesse, a key for David, a star for the daystar, a globe for the nations, a baby for Emmanuel.

At home, this activity could be turned into "O" cookies. Bake sugar cookies in the shape of these symbols. Decorate your tree with them or give them to all who enter your house during the holy days ahead.

Prayers

Prayer for the Feast of Saint Lucy

Preparation: You will need a recorded version of Santa Lucia, *candles in glass containers for the participants, if possible a young girl to volunteer to dress in a white gown with a red sash and a wreath on her head with four unlit candles, and an Advent wreath.*

Leader: Let us be still *pause* and welcome into our presence the long awaited Messiah, Prince of Peace, sign of the impossible, Jesus the Christ.

Santa Lucia *begins to play quietly in the background.*

Leader: And, Saint Lucy, come too! Take a welcome place at our table.

A young woman enters dressed as Saint Lucy she lights two candles on the Advent wreath and stands behind it.

Leader: Let us pray:

Reader: Divine Messiah

source of all light,

give us eyes to see

your kingdom.

Allow us to perceive those things

that are really important during these days of preparation.

Reader: Ancient heroine of Light, Saint Lucy,

guide us when we stray into the darkness

of a world that shuns the Light of the world.

Reader: Jesus, Light of Salvation,

shine in our hearts

so that we may be

brilliant with hope,

sparkling with passion for our faith.

Saint Lucy goes to each participant and lights the candle which they hold. The music plays again.

Leader: Please raise your lighted candles.

Saint Lucy,

receive him, the cause of my devotion.

Receive him, a Light beyond all measure.

Receive him, who never leaves your side.

Saint Lucy leaves as Santa Lucia *plays.*

Leader: Let us take Lucy's light into our heart and homes as we celebrate Incarnation once again.

All: Amen.

Prayer During a Snowstorm
There is a kind of hush
all over the earth.
Deep silence blankets the ground as Spirit whispers
Shhhhhhhhhhhhhhhhhhhhh!
I am making snow for you!
We cannot hear the normal noise of life.
All is muffled in the gentle dance
of endless flakes cascading
in their double-time dance.
Draw me in O Spirit of the Storm.
Let my soul calm into the awestruck silence
of winter's pause.
Every creature has stopped to watch,
huddled closely among one another
to protect the warmth within.
As your white symphony rages,
give me this sacred time
to be alone with you.
May our silent reverie
teach me a little more
or your whimsy,
of your strength,
of your beauty.
Amen.

Connection: If you are privileged to observe a snowstorm, don't just watch from indoors. Bundle up and take a little walk or just stand outdoors. Stop in the silent beauty and see the wonder as a little child.

A Blessing for Families (for the Feast of the Holy Family)

Father: Lord, you are the keeper of my family,
   I offer you praise for your presence in our lives.
   Nothing escapes your gaze.
   Each day you keep us in your care.
   We are grateful for your steadfast love.
   Bless me as the keeper of this family,
   your servant and your imitator,
   I ask the grace and wisdom
   to guide this family ever stronger into faith.

Mother: Jesus, you are the bread of our family life.
   Companion me in my everyday walk.
   You understand the call I share with your mother, Mary.
   May I keep my family with compassion,
       nurturing my family in the spirit of your home at Nazareth.
   May these walls be a sanctuary
   of your presence
   and may the meals we share
   always be a reminder of your love for us.

Child: Holy Spirit, you are our inspiration.
   Keep us aware of each other's needs.
   Help us to bring a spirit of support to one another.
   Let us see each other's gifts.
   Let us nurture one another,
   So that we can become
       All you dream for us to be!

Connection: Celebrate a family meal, a real Sabbath meal, today. Sit at the table and lift a blessing cup of wine (or grape juice) as you say this blessing prayer.

SPECIAL OCCASIONS THROUGHOUT THE YEAR

Every family has special days: birthdays, anniversaries, funerals, graduations, adoptions, and so on. These feasts are high points of celebration within the family. Each occasion is a moment of grace in which we can proclaim the steadfast love of God. A document on family life published by the United States bishops says that our homes and our family units are "the domestic church." Within the walls of our homes our children first experience the breath of God as we celebrate birthdays, holidays, anniversaries, and even funerals. The rhythm of family life teaches that the milestones of our lives together are in the hands of God. Whether we laugh with joy or cry the tears of good-bye, God is with us. When we create special celebrations to affirm those we love, we speak for God who says we are loved and cared for. Our family feasts will be uniquely our own in the way we celebrate them. These are the moments when the original spirit of each household, each heritage is honored. Here are some ideas you might use to celebrate the comings and goings of your family life.

Birthdays

The day of our birth is an anniversary of life. Each year this day stands apart as a moment to reverence our life and the lives of those we love. We should take special care in the way we celebrate. The following are some ways to keep holy this day of life:

Eight Ways to Celebrate Your Day (F)
1. Don't just let the day happen. Plan to do something you enjoy on your birthday.
2. Send flowers to your parents. Thank them for giving you life.
3. Give yourself a gift, something no one knows you would like.
4. Look up on your birth certificate the exact moment of your birth.

When that time comes, pause and pray silently for the gift of your life.

5. Donate a book to a school library in your name.

6. Plant a tree for your sake and the sake of the earth.

7. Call on the phone someone from your childhood, perhaps your "best friend" in grade school or a favorite coach or teacher.

8. Take some time off and visit a favorite place: a park, the zoo, a museum. Take the whole family or go alone, but relax and enjoy your day.

Half Birthday (F)

If a member of your family has a birthday during Christmastime or a child has a summer birthday and never celebrates with schoolmates, consider celebrating a half birthday. Six months after the birthday, have a one-half celebration: Serve a cake that has icing on only one side, give one half of your gift (one sock, one glove, one half of a deck of cards), give one half of a birthday card, blow balloons up only half way, sing the first half of "Happy Birthday," take a group photograph of the partygoers from the waist down.

Birthday Placemat (F)

What a waste it is to throw away the notes and cards we receive at birthdays. Create a placemat for a child or elderly birthday person. Create a collage of the cards and interesting facts from the day's newspaper. Arrange them on a piece of construction paper (11 x 16). Place the paper between two pieces of clear self-adhesive vinyl.

Special Place Setting (F)

To distinguish your birthday person, serve the day's meals on special birthday dinnerware. This place setting should be a unique, one-of-a-kind item. You could purchase a place setting of china, utensils, a glass, and a napkin in the housewares department of a store or get creative at a thrift store or antique shop. This single table setting is used only on a birthday. This project makes a great gift for someone who lives alone, or as a gift for a family.

Child's Hope Chest (F)
On a child's first birthday give a good-sized chest or footlocker. Each year add a gift for their future: a Bible, a dictionary, an antique from a family member, a handmade quilt. The treasures in the chest will become a priceless heritage.

A Birthday Prayer
Timeless Creator,
I honor the day
of my first cry,
sucking deep the sweet air of life.
Year upon year
time pervades my soul
leaving a story
of memories.
I stand in You now
filled with gratitude
and sweet delight.
Learning the
ways of eternity.

Vacations

Vacations can be a blessing or a curse depending on how well prepared you are. Little things can make all the difference. Planning your activities and travel is an important part of your preparation. Here are some simple suggestions that can make this adventure even more fun than you expected.

The Casserole Club (F)
Enlist other families to commit to the Christian concern, "When I was hungry, you gave me to eat." Trade names and vacation dates. On the night your chosen family is returning from their vacation, drop off a prepared casserole supper for them. In turn, when you arrive home, you will be treated to the same luxury.

Travel Journal (F)

Keep a journal of each day of your trip. Include humorous moments, quotes like, "At 8:30 AM, Jason says for the fifth time 'Are we there yet?'" This collection of reflections will be a treasured diary in years to come.

Jelly Roll Pan Desk (F)

For each child in the family prepare a lap desk. Buy a jelly roll pan (it can later be recycled for kitchen use), and fill it with pencils, pens, scissors, crayons, paper, and puzzle books. The pan provides a perfect lap desk and the raised edge prevents items from falling off the tray.

The Hundred-Mile Gift (F)

If you are driving with young children, it is difficult to keep them amused for the long drive. For each hundred-mile stretch prepare a small plastic sandwich bag with a surprise in it. As the odometer marks the passing of the hundred miles present the children with a bag. Surprises can include a small toy, a deck of cards or travel game, cookies, or sunglasses. This simple plan encourages children to look forward to each milestone and the time passes quickly.

Christmas in July (F)

Plan to purchase or create a vacation Christmas ornament for the family's Christmas tree. Each year look for a little symbol of your vacation, perhaps some miniature replica of something you saw or something distinctive to the area. Attach a hook and the date of the trip and add it to your tree next Christmas.

Vacation Box (F)

Bring an empty box (plain or fancy) on your trip. As you travel fill the box with mementos of the trip: postcards, little souvenirs, match covers, a pretty rock or shell. When you return home, display the box so you can easily revisit your vacation.

Money Buckets (F)

Spending too much on a trip is a common pitfall. In order to conserve and allow children to understand the value of money, prepare a vacation allowance for each child. Decide together what would be an appropriate amount for each "bucket." Take a small container (an empty yogurt cup works well) and give each child this container filled with the allowance. This money is strictly for their souvenirs and special treats.

Color-Coded Fun (F)

Buy everyone on the trip the same color caps or T-shirts. Plan to wear them when visiting crowded tourist spots. It is much easier to find a wandering three-year-old in a bright red cap than a bareheaded child!

Camera Fun (F)

Give each vacationer a disposable camera to chronicle the trip. This gesture will insure plenty of photos of everyone having fun. In addition, you will receive a variety of versions of the same trip.

Coming Home From Vacation Prayer

Lord of Leisure,
bless my return.
The house is waiting for the activity of daily life,
but I yearn to stay away at leisure and play.
So, give me the grace of a holy return.
Fill my heart with memories of everything
that delighted me during this vacation.
Allow me moments of day dreaming
back to the joy of absolute leisure.
In the winter of my discontent
teach me to harbor the sweet vision of my rest.
Amen.

Death

Death of a Pet (F)

When a beloved goldfish or an elderly cat finally succumbs to death, it is difficult for children to understand and accept the loss. This occasion is a perfect opportunity to teach children the ritual and process of letting go of someone they love. It is never a good idea to dispose of the animal without ceremony. This is an occasion for a funeral. Burial can be done with great flourish (or with a great flush, in the case of a goldfish). Gather the family and gently put to rest the family's old friend. Let each family member throw a shovel of dirt into the hole and share a favorite memory of old Buster's or Samantha's life. After the hole is filled say this simple prayer:

God of all creation,
we thank you for the life of_____(pet's name).
He/she was a wonderful companion
and we will miss his/her presence.
Help us to remember the good memories
we have of _____(pet's name).
Please touch our grieving hearts
as we bury our pet.
She/he gave us the gifts of faithfulness and joy.
These gifts will stay in our hearts even as we say good-bye.
Amen.

Find a large rock and a little paint and allow the children to create a tombstone for their lost friend. You may even wish to designate a certain area in your yard as a pet cemetery. During your family's stay in the home, this little corner will be well filled with God's creatures who have accompanied you on life's journey.

Death of a Relative or Friend (F)

The loss of a well-loved elderly relative, particularly a grandparent, can devastate a family. It is not enough simply to acknowledge this passing. It is particularly dangerous not to include children in the funeral. It is important for them to accompany their parents to the services and burial. This is an occasion to proclaim our belief in eternal life.

A simple exercise to help a child grieve is to ask them to write a good-bye letter or draw a picture expressing their memories of and feelings for the deceased person. Let this be personal and private.

Death of a Child (F)

One of the most difficult moments in family life is the loss of a child. Whether through miscarriage, stillbirth, or the death of a young family member, the darkness that pervades the lives of the family is overpowering. Siblings have an especially difficult time comprehending the sudden absence of a beloved brother or sister.

So often when a child dies, friends and relatives feel awkward talking about the child's life. Yet nothing consoles a grieving family more than stories about this child. One way to do this is through an album of photographs, remembrances, and stories about the child.

Another excellent expression of grief and sympathy is to plant a tree in memory of the child. Flowering or ornamental trees are particularly appropriate; every spring proclaims a beautiful reminder of the precious life. A small plaque could be mounted on the tree, like one a friend found when she moved into a new home: "Danny's Tree." Danny, an infant of the previous owner, died of Sudden Infant Death Syndrome. Every spring as Danny's tree blooms the home's new family prays for Danny and his family.

Visiting the Cemetery (F)

Long after the funeral service is over we may need to confront our loss more privately. A visit to the cemetery can be a therapeutic way to remember and grieve. On Memorial Day many families enjoy the custom of placing flowers on the graves of all of their deceased family members.

Elderly people who no longer drive find it difficult to visit the cemetery. As a wonderful corporal work of mercy you might want to drive
an elderly widow or widower to a spouse's grave with a fresh bouquet.
Try to remember special occasions when your offer would be most
meaningful, such as a wedding anniversary or a spouse's birthday.

Prayer for a Difficult Time
The Narrow Gate
O, Lordly Lord,
the narrow gate is not good news.
I much prefer the wider gate,
the easy way.
Let me move into the kingdom
with the crowd.
Just moving along,
singing my song.
Why do you keep pointing
to the singular
path?
Why are you so insistent?
It must be that love
requires such a choice.
Narrow gates require
determination,
courage, and
deliberate grace.
While I would rather not,
I love you too much
to do anything other than
follow you
through
narrow gates,
through uphill paths,

through dark woods,
through steep cliffs,
through Calvary,
through a tomb,
into unending joy.

Connection: Think of someone you know who is going through a tough time in their lives (illness, divorce, grief, loss of employment). Pray for them today and take time to visit and encourage them for the sake of the "narrow gate."

ABOUT THE AUTHOR

Jeanne Hunt is director of product development for the institutional market for St. Anthony Messenger Press where she contributes to *Bringing Home the Word, Homily Helps, Catholic Update, Every Day Catholic,* and *Faith Formation Update* and can be heard on American Catholic Radio. She holds degrees in art and theology and has served as director of family life for the archdiocese of Cincinnati and been a director of religious education for many years. She gives workshops for catechists and teachers and preaches at parish missions and retreats on faith formation. She wrote *Choir Prayers* and *Handing on the Faith: When You Are a Single Parent.*